Dancing in the Dragon's Jaws

Also by Graeme Carlé and published by
Emmaus Road Publishing

Eating Sacred Cows
A Closer Look at Tithing

Because of the Angels
Unveiling 1 Corinthians 11:2-16

The Red Heifer's Ashes
Mysteries of Ancient Israel

Born of the Spirit
A study guide for new believers

The Revelation series:
1. Dancing in the Dragon's Jaws
The Mystery of Israel's Survival

2. Slouching Towards Bethlehem
The Rise of the Antichrists

3. Gotta Serve Somebody
The Mystery the Marks & 666

4. Silencing the Witnesses
Jerusalem & the Ascent of Secularism

Dancing in the Dragon's Jaws

The Mystery of Israel's Survival

Graeme Carlé

First published 2011, revised 2013, 2018
Illustrations by Alyssa McClelland

ISBN 978-0-9582746-5-4

Book title inspired by the album
Dancing In The Dragon's Jaws
by Bruce Cockburn
© 1979 Golden Mountain Music Corp. (SOCAN)
Used with permission.

Photo of Arch of Titus by Philip Church.
Used with permission.

Unless otherwise stated, all Scripture quoted is from
the NEW AMERICAN STANDARD BIBLE®, Copyright ©1995
The Lockman Foundation. Used with permission.

International listing 2018 by Ingram Content
with the assistance of Wild Side Publishing
www.wildsidepublishing.com

Published by Emmaus Road Publishing
PO Box 38 823 Howick, Auckland 2014 New Zealand
www.emmausroad.org.nz

To Dorothy Carlé

Thanks
There are so many I want to thank for their help and encouragement. The most obvious – Marcus Ardern, Barbara McConchie, David Lee, Olivia Ladyman, Elizabeth Rowe, John Stringer, Alistair Reese, Peter Maddison, Arthur Amon, Simone & Steve Varney, Oliver Carlé, Jono Smith, Marie Shaw, Alyssa McClelland, Peter Aranyi, Dave & Anneliejse Dobbyn, the whole SPHNKS class (*Society for the Prevention of Hillsiders Not Knowing Stuff*), Western Suburbs Christian Fellowship in Wellington.

Contents

Introduction

The nation of Israel is one of the greatest mysteries of all time. Only 21,000 square kilometres or 8,000 square miles, Israel is less than a third the size of Sri Lanka, half of Switzerland, a tenth of New Zealand or the British Isles, or one fourteenth of the state of California. How can such a tiny nation make such an impact as to be almost daily in the world's headlines?

And how can any people be utterly devastated so many times for almost four thousand years and still exist? The descendants of one man named Jacob (later renamed Israel), this family of twelve sons grew to one and a half million during four hundred years of slavery in Egypt before spending forty years as refugees in the wilderness of Sinai and Arabia.[1] After finally conquering the promised land of Canaan, the fledgling nation was then itself conquered over the next thousand years by the successive great empires of the Assyrians, Babylonians, Medo-Persians, Greeks and Romans.

Each of these at some stage tried to annihilate or assimilate the Jewish people but each time this tiny nation was somehow reestablished. The extraordinarily brutal attempt in 70 AD by Titus and the Roman legions left over one million dead, Jerusalem and the fabulous Temple in

---

[1] It now seems the traditional location of Mt. Sinai as sanctified in about 325 AD by Helena, mother of the emperor Constantine, is wrong; it may actually be across the Gulf of Aqaba in today's Saudi Arabia. *The Biblical Significance of Jabal al-Lawz*, Charles A. Whittaker www.newprovidencebc.com/Mt%20Sinai/Biblical%20significance%20of%20Jabal%20al%20Lawz.pdf, 28 Mar, 2009

ashes, and the survivors in an exile that was to last for the next two thousand years.

Even in exile the Jews were singled out for persecution and death. The Inquisition of the Middle Ages and the later pogroms of Eastern Europe culminated just sixty years ago in Hitler's holocaust of six million more Jewish men, women and children, one third of all Jews alive at the time. Of course, Hitler also brutally eliminated eight million other 'undesirables' from the Third Reich including the handicapped, gypsies and homosexuals, but he marked out the Jews alone to be destroyed in their entirety – every Jewish man, woman and child. In Winston Churchill's summation: 'There is no doubt that this is probably the greatest and most horrible crime ever committed in the whole history of the world, and it has been done by scientific machinery by nominally civilised men in the name of a great State and one of the leading races of Europe.' [2]

Yet just three years later, on May 14, 1948, Israel was reborn as a nation! Fifty years earlier, the ancient Hebrew language had been revived and within twenty years, in the Six Day War of 1967, the Jewish people finally regained their ancient capital, Jerusalem. Israel exists today as a sovereign people, with their own language, in their own land, possessing again their holy city.

How can this be?

There is no shortage of theories – Edward Said writes in *The Question of Palestine* of the 'enormous, hopelessly proliferating mass of writing on the Middle East generally

---

[2] Sir Martin Gilbert, *Churchill And The Jews*, London; Simon & Shuster, 2007, p. 215

and on the Palestinians, Zionism, and their conflict in particular.'³ Even amongst those who believe Israel were the Chosen of God, the legitimacy of the nation's existence today is debated, many believing that Israel was replaced by the church in the first century because they failed to recognise Jesus of Nazareth as their Messiah. 'There is no mention of the land of Israel in the New Testament', they say, and thus no Christian basis for Jewish claims to the holy land.

However, the mystery of Israel's existence is most clearly revealed and explained in a series of visions received in about 100 AD by a prisoner, John son of Zebedee (and one of the twelve apostles), in exile on the Isle of Patmos. Not only do these ancient visions explain exactly what has been happening and the hidden divine purpose, but they also predict what will ultimately happen to Israel. This book examines one of John's visions – as recorded in chapter 12 of the *Book of Revelation*.

The visions of Revelation have largely been lost to modern readers. Popular electronic encyclopedia *Encarta 96* succinctly describes the problem:

> In communicating to his fellow Christians 'what you see, what is and what is to take place hereafter' (Rev 1:19), the author deliberately chose a literary vehicle that would tend to conceal his message from the enemies of the church. This vehicle was the apocalypse, a Jewish literary form characterized by an often elaborately symbolic interpretation and prediction of events. The apocalyptic symbols of Revelation are derived from prophetic books of the Old Testament and from the common Christian tradition.

---

³ *The Question of Palestine*, London; Vintage, 1992, p. 245

No doubt the earliest readers of the book understood its visions and imagery, but in the centuries since Revelation was written, the key to the original meaning of its symbolism was lost. Efforts to recover it have produced widely divergent systems of interpretation but no general recognition of any one system as nearest to the author's meaning. Apart from its religious message, Revelation continues to be valued today for its magnificent literary qualities and for its historical depiction of a crisis in Christianity.

As *Encarta* says, there is 'no doubt the earliest readers of the book understood its visions and imagery' and many believe that 'in the centuries since Revelation was written, the key to the original meaning of its symbolism was lost'. However, as the writer also notes, 'the apocalyptic symbols of Revelation are derived from prophetic books of the Old Testament and from the common Christian tradition'. This is indeed the key but it has never been lost – we still have the 'prophetic books of the Old Testament' and all essential 'common Christian tradition' was recorded for us in the New Testament. The key has simply not been recognised or applied sufficiently.

You do not have to take my word for anything in this book – I have included all the references so that you can check everything for yourself. It may seem a lot of work but it is fascinating and inspiring. You can also look for supernatural help because the same Holy Spirit who inspired 'the earliest readers of the book' can just as surely inspire us:

> the Helper, the Holy Spirit, whom the Father will send in My name, He will teach you all things, and bring to your remembrance all that I said to you. (John 14:26)

All we have to do is ask Him to teach and remind us before we begin. Then, put the key we find into the lock by identifying and establishing at every point the original meaning of each of the symbols and see what opens up.

Revelation 12

1. And a great sign appeared in heaven: a woman clothed with the sun, and the moon under her feet, and on her head a crown of twelve stars;

2. and she was with child; and she cried out, being in labour and in pain to give birth.

3. And another sign appeared in heaven: and behold, a great red dragon having seven heads and ten horns, and on his heads were seven diadems.

4. And his tail swept a third of the stars of heaven, and threw them to the earth. And the dragon stood before the woman who was about to give birth, so that when she gave birth he might devour her child.

5. And she gave birth to a son, a male child, who is to rule all the nations with a rod of iron; and her child was caught up to God and to His throne.

6. And the woman fled into the wilderness where she had a place prepared by God, so that there she might be nourished for one thousand two hundred and sixty days.

7. And there was war in heaven; Michael and his angels waging war with the dragon. And the dragon and his angels waged war

8. and they were not strong enough, and there was no longer a place found for them in heaven.

9. And the great dragon was thrown down, the serpent of old who is called the devil and Satan, who deceives the whole world; he was thrown down to the earth, and his angels were thrown down with him.

10. And I heard a loud voice in heaven, saying: 'Now the salvation, and the power, and the kingdom of our God and the authority of His Christ have come, for the accuser of our brethren has been thrown down, who accuses them before our God day and night.

11. And they overcame him because of the blood of the Lamb and because of the word of their testimony, and they did not love their life even to death.

12. For this reason, rejoice, O heavens and you who dwell in them. Woe to the earth and the sea, because the devil has come down to you, having great wrath, knowing that he only has a short time'.

13. And when the dragon saw that he was thrown down to the earth, he persecuted the woman who gave birth to the male child.

14. And the two wings of a great eagle were given to the woman, in order that she might fly into the wilderness to her place, where she was nourished for a time and times and half a time, from the presence of the serpent.

15. And the serpent poured water like a river out of his mouth after the woman, so that he might cause her to be swept away with the flood.

16. And the earth helped the woman, and the earth opened its mouth and drank up the river which the dragon poured out of his mouth.

17. And the dragon was enraged with the woman, and went off to make war with the rest of her offspring, who keep the commandments of God and hold to the testimony of Jesus.

We see here three primary figures – the woman, her child and the dragon. They are locked in some kind of cosmic battle that ends with angels casting the dragon and his angels down to the earth. There are also three natural divisions in the vision: the first six verses have the woman giving birth and then fleeing into the wilderness; vv. 7-12 reveal the heavenly outcome and vv. 13-17 the earthly outcome.

The three figures require careful study because John says the mother and child are a 'great sign' (vv. 1-2), or of huge significance, as is the great red dragon (v. 3). In fact, the woman is today so widely misunderstood that this vision

                    Dancing in the Dragon's Jaws

has been rendered incomprehensible. Like putting the first shirt button in the wrong button hole, this misunderstanding has displaced everything that follows, hence the vision has been largely set aside as irrelevant.

1. The Pregnant Woman

Israel before Jesus

So who is this woman, clothed with the sun, with the moon under her feet, and crowned with twelve stars? She is obviously symbolic. Some see her as a pagan goddess, crowned with the twelve signs of the zodiac, even though there is no reference to this anywhere in the text. Others see her as Mary, the mother of Jesus, giving birth to Him. This is the most widely held view, being the official teaching of the Roman Catholic Church and so theoretically has over one billion adherents or 20% of the earth's population. The twelve stars are assumed to symbolise angels through a cross-reference to Revelation 1:20 where 'the mystery of the seven stars' is explained as meaning 'the angels of the seven churches.' One result of this interpretation in New Zealand is Wellington's central city church building named St. Mary of the Angels with twelve stars graven in stone on its foundations (see photo 1).

The crown of stars is then assumed to reveal Mary as the 'Queen of the Angels' and this belief has permeated our world much more than we may realise. Consider, for example, the full original name of one of the world's most famous cities: 'El Pueblo de Nuestra Senora la Reina de Los Angeles de Portiuncula.' Translating from Spanish as 'The Village of Our Lady the Queen of the Angels of Portiuncula', you can easily understand why it has been shortened to 'Los Angeles' or to just 'L.A.' Often referred to as 'the City of Angels', it was actually named after Mary as their queen.

Photo 1 — St Mary of the Angels, Wellington, New Zealand. Note the crown of twelve stars motif.

This regal authority is portrayed, particularly in Latin America, by innumerable icons showing her holding her little baby out of harm's way while she stands victorious over the dragon. This has led many to believe they should cast out demons in Mary's name rather than in Jesus' name (cf. Mark 16:17). In 1849 Pope Pius IX issued an encyclical stating, 'her foot has crushed the head of Satan'[4] and teaching that 'God placed Mary far above all the angels and saints and so filled her with every heavenly grace from his own divine treasury so that her innocence and holiness exceeded every creature but God himself'.[5]

[4] www.ewtn.com/library/ENCYC/P9UBIPR2.HTM, 19 Jan 2009.
This was based on an admitted mistranslation of Genesis 3:15
www.catholic.com/thisrock/1997/9709chap. asp, 19 Jan 2009
[5] www.opusangelorum.org/Formation/Maryregina.html, 15 Dec 2008

A hundred years later, Pius XII (Pope from 1939 to 1958) added that 'when the glorious Virgin Mary entered triumphantly into heaven and was elevated above the choirs of angels to the throne of the Most Holy Trinity', her Son Jesus 'placed a triple crown of glory on her head, presented her to the heavenly court, seated her at his right hand and pronounced her Queen of the Universe.' He explained that Jesus, 'after asserting that all power was given to Him in heaven and on earth, gave His mother a share in His glory, His majesty, His kingship because she was associated with Him as mother and minister in His work of redemption' so that 'Mary is likewise associated with Christ forever with infinite power.' Her kingdom is not only 'as vast as her Son's, since nothing of His kingdom is excluded from hers,' but also 'the Church salutes her as sovereign and as Queen of the Angels and Queen of the Universe and encourages us to invoke her day and night'.[6]

Now, of course, if any of this was true, it would be of huge significance to us all, just as John says of his vision. However, if the woman is to be Mary, we then have to establish when exactly she fled into the wilderness from the dragon's wrath for one thousand, two hundred and sixty days (v. 6). Similarly, when was she given two wings of the great eagle to fly into the wilderness to her place (v. 14)? The idea that this refers to her Assumption (or her being taken up bodily into heaven) has the wrong destination – how can the wilderness be heaven? The timing is also wrong – how can this only be for three and a half years? And when did the dragon try to sweep her away with a river out of his

---

[6] www.opusangelorum.org/Formation/Maryregina.html, 15 Dec 2008

                    Dancing in the Dragon's Jaws

mouth (v. 15)? The Bible tells us nothing like this in regard to Mary.

There are several other possible interpretations [7] but there is a far better option for us.

Rather than guess at possibilities, we can actually use the key identified in Encarta as being found in the 'prophetic books of the Old Testament and in the common Christian tradition' which was recorded for us in the New Testament. If we will take the proper time necessary to understand the details John gives us in this vision, we will see it demonstrates an important principle of Biblical interpretation:

> The unfolding of Your words gives light; it gives understanding to the simple. (Psa 119:130)

Since Revelation was the last book of the Scriptures to be written, all earlier references to these symbols and their interpretations should be understood first – 'the unfolding' of these sheds remarkable light.

---

[7] For example, some teach the woman is the church. Since the church did not exist before Christ, this means the child cannot be Jesus but in their view it becomes a later select company of believers known as 'overcomers' who will not flee when the non-overcoming church flees into the wilderness (v. 14). Others teach that the woman represents the faithful of both old and new covenants throughout the ages but what then are we to make of the dragon's attack on 'the rest of her offspring' (v. 17)? Are they believers too? If so, why are they not included in the woman? If unbelievers, why would the dragon attack them more than other unbelievers? Still others take the woman as Israel, the child as the overcomers and the rest of the children as end-time saints (e.g. http://www.restoringthevision.com/Ch12RtheV.htm, 1 May 2009)

The Sun, Moon and Twelve Stars

There are many references in the Scriptures to the sun, moon and stars but only one specifies twelve stars: Joseph's dream. Joseph, one of Jacob's twelve sons, had the dream in about 1900 BC but the early Christians would have known about it because the first generation of the church were all Jews, proselytes (non-Jews who had converted) or taught by Jewish leaders (Acts 2:10 & 42).

Joseph was Jacob's favourite son and was given the famous multicoloured coat (as popularised in the musical, *Joseph and The Amazing Technicolor Dream Coat*) which made his eleven brothers murderously jealous. Joseph actually had two parallel dreams[8] prophesying his family's future but we are only concerned here with the details of the second:

> Now he had still another dream, and related it to his brothers, and said, 'Lo, I have had still another dream; and behold, the sun and the moon and eleven stars were bowing down to me' (Gen 37:9)

Although there are only eleven stars at this stage, vv. 10-11 continue:

> And he related it to his father and to his brothers; and his father rebuked him and said to him, 'What is this dream that you have had? Shall I and your mother and your brothers actually come to bow ourselves down before you to the ground?'
> And his brothers were jealous of him, but his father kept the saying in mind.

Notice, Jacob gives us the inspired interpretation of the dream: Jacob is the sun, Joseph's mother Rachel is the moon

---

[8] See also Genesis 37:5-8

and Joseph's eleven brothers are the stars. In John's vision, therefore, the twelfth star is Joseph because he is the twelfth son.

As we will now see, all three of these symbols identify the woman as *the nation of Israel.*

(i) 'A crown of twelve stars'

Joseph's prophetic dream was literally fulfilled some twenty years later in Egypt after he had become governor of Egypt and his brothers, not recognising him, bowed down before him (Gen 42:6-9; 43:26-29). Over the next four hundred years in Egypt, the family of twelve sons grew into the nation of twelve tribes. The symbolic use of stars for all the children of Israel comes from God's promise to Abraham 'to multiply your descendants as the stars of the heavens' (Gen 22:17. Also Gen 15:5) and again to Isaac (Gen 26:4). John's vision, therefore, refers to the nation of Israel from its earliest beginnings.

As for the woman wearing a 'crown', the Greek word used [9] denotes not a queenly crown but one worn by a winning athlete or a bride, signifying not her authority but her identity. This crown of twelve stars therefore reveals her not as ruling over angels but as being the twelve tribes of Israel, called and set apart for a particular task from her beginning.

---

[9] The Greek, *stephanos*, contrasts with the 'diadems' (Gk *diadema*) worn by the seven heads of the dragon (v. 3). In English, crown and diadem can be used as synonyms but not in Greek. W.E. Vine's *Expository Dictionary of New Testament Words* (p. 258) explains that '*stephanos* is never used as *diadema* is' – *stephanos* denotes 'a reward or prize' as won by athletes or 'a token of public honour', whether for distinguished service or celebration of weddings and feasts. It is 'an emblem of life, joy, reward and glory (e.g. Phil 4:1; 1 Thess 2:19; Jas 1:12; Rev 2:10; 3:11; 4:4, 10)… and triumph (Rev 6:2; 9:7; 12:1)'. *Diadema*, however, is 'always the symbol of kingly or imperial dignity' i.e. authority.

(ii) 'Clothed with the sun'

In Joseph's dream, Jacob is the sun but in John's vision, the woman is described as 'clothed with the sun.' Biblically, to clothe someone is to provide or restore an identity e.g. the high priest (Ex 28:2-3, Zech 3:1-7). Or remember how the father reclothed the prodigal son in Luke 15:22?[10]

The woman being 'clothed with the sun' therefore means that she is to be identified with or bears the name of the 'sun', the patriarch Jacob whose name was later changed to Israel (Gen 32:28). She is the personification of the nation of Israel from its very beginning, confirming the testimony of 'the twelve stars.'

(iii) 'The moon under her feet'

In Joseph's dream, the moon was his mother Rachel but this in itself is mysterious because she could never bow before him, having earlier died giving birth to his younger brother Benjamin (Gen 35:18). Jacob clearly saw this as significant because instead of rejecting it as impossible, he 'kept the saying in mind' (v. 11).

Rachel's terrible labour became proverbial in Israel so that over a thousand years later, when Jeremiah speaks of the nation of Israel being in great distress because of the Babylonian invasion, he describes their national lamentation as 'Rachel is weeping for her children' (Jer 31:15). Some six hundred years later again, during the Roman occupation, Matthew quotes this proverb to describe the nation's mourning after Herod had slaughtered all the male babies

---

[10] The Greek verb, *enduo* to clothe, has entered the English language as to endue, meaning to 'furnish person with powers, qualities, etc'. (*Concise Oxford Dictionary*, p. 318). The same concept comes from Latin (*vestis* clothing), giving us investiture and 'to invest', meaning 'to clothe, endue person with qualities, insignia of office, rank, etc.'

and toddlers in Bethlehem at the time of Jesus' birth (Matt 2:16-18).

We find then that 'Rachel' is a metaphor for the nation of Israel in deep distress in any generation. It is particularly appropriate in John's vision because the woman is 'about to give birth' and her baby is in grave danger. As for 'the moon under her feet', Israeli women sat on birth stools to give birth while the midwives knelt at their feet to receive the baby (Gen 30:3, Ex 1:16) so the moon, Rachel, being under this woman's feet signifies that he will be born in the land of Israel.

In summary then, the woman is shown by all three identifying features, the sun, the moon and the twelve stars, to be the nation of Israel, called and set apart by God for a particular task.

'She Cried Out ...'

Now we see that task, unique to her as a nation among all the nations – the woman 'cried out, being in labour and in pain to give birth' (v. 2). Her labour pains also were unique and included her going into exile in Babylon as predicted in about 720 BC by the prophet, Micah:

> Writhe and labour to give birth, daughter of Zion,
> Like a woman in childbirth,
> For now you will go out of the city, dwell in the field, and
> go to Babylon.
> There you will be rescued; there the LORD will redeem
> you
> From the hand of your enemies (Mic 4:10)

In this remarkable prophecy, Micah is predicting over one hundred years beforehand the agony of Israel's being conquered and taken into exile by the Babylonians from about 600 BC and their eventual rescue (which occurred seventy years after that). This exile was due to Israel's sin but God still had a plan for rescuing them:

> 3. Therefore, He will give them up until the time when she who is in labor has borne a child.
> Then the remainder of His brethren will return to the sons of Israel.
> 4. And He will arise and shepherd His flock in the strength of the LORD,
> In the majesty of the name of the LORD His God.
> And they will remain, because at that time He will be great to the ends of the earth.
> 5. And this One will be our peace. (Mic 5:3-5)

Israel's unique role and glory among all the nations is to give birth to 'a child' (v. 3) – this is her *raison d'etre*, her eternal purpose or destiny.

The Child

So who is this child? Look at the preceding verse in Micah 5:

> 2. But as for you, Bethlehem Ephrathah…[11]
> From you One will go forth for Me to be ruler in Israel.
> His goings forth are from long ago
> From the days of eternity.
> 3. Therefore, He will give them up until the time
> When she who is in labor has borne a child…

This prediction of Micah's is one of the most famous of all the messianic prophecies. There is nothing vague about the identity of this child: born in Bethlehem, He is from

---

[11] This village, about ten kilometres southwest of Jerusalem, was already famous as the place of Rachel's agonising labour and burial (Gen 35:19) and as David's birthplace (1 Sam 17:12). The qualifying name is to distinguish it from another Bethlehem in northern Israel (Josh 19:15)

David's line in Judah 'to be ruler' of the nation of Israel; His coming was planned long ago, 'from the days of eternity.' He is Jesus.

Micah is therefore telling 'the daughter of Zion', or the nation of Israel, that as painful as her captivity will be in Babylon, her travail will eventually bring forth Messiah. So, returning to Revelation 12, from both Joseph's dream and Micah's prophecy, we have a well-established meaning for the archetypal mother and child: *the woman is the nation of Israel from the very beginning of her calling, and her child is Messiah.*

'A Rod of Iron'

> And she gave birth to a son, a male child, who is to rule all the nations with a rod of iron; and her child was caught up to God and to His throne (Rev 12:5)

John here refers to another ancient messianic prophecy. In Psalm 2, written about 1000 BC, God the Father says:

> 6. 'But as for Me, I have installed My king upon Zion, My holy mountain.
> 7. '… You are my Son; today I have begotten You.
> 8. Ask of Me, and I will surely give the nations as Your inheritance,
> And the very ends of the earth as Your possession.
> 9. You will break them with a rod of iron,
> You will shatter them like earthenware'

Zion was David's citadel so this confirms Messiah is of the house of David. He is to rule not only Israel but also 'the nations' or Gentiles.[12] His 'inheritance' is to extend from Mt. Zion in Jerusalem to 'the very ends of the earth.' Literally, this is to the bottom of the South Pacific where New Zealand finally heard the gospel in 1814. There remain a few nations in between still to hear of Him.

The analogy of a rod shattering the earthenware is an ancient one – if a potter did not like how his pot turned out from the kiln, he broke it. We see this clearly in a prophetic drama which Jeremiah was commanded to enact. He had to buy a potter's earthenware jar and break it in front of the leaders of Israel, saying:

> Thus says the LORD of hosts, 'Just so shall I break this people and this city, even as one breaks a potter's vessel, which cannot again be repaired…' (Jer 19:1-13).

In the same way, Messiah is given such authority and such power over all the nations of the earth, He can ultimately do whatever He likes with them. Happily, He is loving and gentle as well as all-powerful, but, ultimately, He will judge everyone (2 Cor 5:10). In the meantime, He allows us time to willingly submit to Him:

> All authority has been given to Me in heaven and on earth. Go therefore and make disciples of all the nations… teaching them to observe all that I have commanded you; and remember, I am with you always, even to the end of the age (Matt 28:18-20)

---

[12] For any who may not know, 'Gentile' simply means non-Jewish, being a translation of the Hebrew *goy* (plural *goyim*) and the Greek *ethnos* which literally means 'race or nation.' The English translators of the Bible therefore use 'Gentiles' and 'nations' interchangeably.

Except for Paul, the Early Church took many years to understand the magnificence and full extent of God's intentions, being 'slow of heart to believe in all that the prophets had spoken' (Luke 24:25). Many continued to think that Jesus had come to Israel only, not seeing that Messiah's 'rod of iron' is to rule all the nations, so in Revelation 12:5 John reminds them again.

The second half of our text, Revelation 12:5b ('And her child was caught up to God and to His throne'), describes the resurrection and ascension of Jesus and we will come to that soon.

The Timing

We have to understand the context of this vision, about 100 AD, to grasp its full significance.

The Romans had destroyed Israel as a nation in 70 AD so the churches needed to know God's intentions for the Jews, and for the nation of Israel. Did they still have a future? Or did this judgment mean He had finished with them forever, because they had rejected their Messiah? John, being the last survivor of the original twelve apostles, is writing to reveal God's intentions. He is also confirming in pictorial form what Paul had earlier written in doctrinal form in Romans, chapters 9-11.

It is also important to understand the time-span of this vision so far: the woman symbolises the nation of Israel from its beginning in about 1900 BC; her Child was born around 5 BC so these first five verses of Revelation 12 cover two thousand years of Jewish history. They also provide, as we will see, an extraordinary overview of the entire Old Testament or *Tanakh*, as the Jews call it.

2. The Dragon

'China?'

So far we have seen God's plan for Messiah and Israel's being set apart to fulfil that plan. We now see the opposition to it through the third figure in the vision:

> 3. And another sign appeared in heaven: and behold, a great red dragon having seven heads and ten horns, and on his heads were seven diadems.
> 4. And his tail swept away a third of the stars of heaven, and threw them to the earth. And the dragon stood before the woman who was about to give birth, so that when she gave birth he might devour her child.

'A great red dragon', another 'sign' or mystery, is trying to kill the child and sweeps away 'a third of the stars of heaven'. Today, most people immediately associate the dragon with the Chinese, due to their colourful dragon-dances and dragon-boat races as well as the dragon being the sacred symbol of the Emperor of China. However, many cultures have dragons in their mythology, from the ancient Egyptians, Greeks, Romans, Scandinavians, British and Germans to the Aztecs and the Moche people of pre-Columbian Peru (whose ceramics of dragons date to about 100 AD). In most instances, the dragons represent primal forces of nature or the universe and are associated with wisdom and longevity.

However, the Scriptures give us a very different perspective:

> And the great dragon was thrown down, the serpent of old who is called the devil and Satan, who deceives the

> whole world; he was thrown down to the earth, and his angels were thrown down with him. (Rev 12:9)

The dragon symbolises a spiritual being, the devil, and this vision describes one of his visible manifestations so that we can identify this otherwise invisible enemy of God and mankind. Not only is he 'the serpent of old' who tempted Adam and Eve while 'disguising himself as an angel of light' (2 Cor 11:3 & 14, Ezek 28:12-17) but he is also a 'great red dragon, having seven heads and ten horns'.

He is 'red' because in the Biblical Middle East, that was considered the colour of the earth. For example, the name Adam, or man, literally means ruddy or red and Esau, who was born notably 'ruddy' (Gen 25:25), later was renamed Edom when he ate 'that red stuff', or lentils (Gen 25:30). Today's American state of Colorado received its name of Red Colour from the Spanish after its red earth. The 'great red dragon' is therefore revealed here as taking on huge form *in the earth and through mankind*.

'Seven Heads and Ten Horns'

Many have failed to grasp the significance of the dragon's seven heads and ten horns because they are not immediately explained. In fact, John himself did not get it until they had appeared twice more, as he records in Revelation 13 and 17. In chapter 13, they are on a beast or wild animal:[13]

> And I saw a beast coming up out of the sea, having ten horns and seven heads, and on his horns were ten diadems and on his heads were blasphemous names (Rev 13:1)

---

[13] Greek, *therion* 'almost invariably denotes a wild beast', *Expository Dictionary of New Testament Words*, W.E. Vine, p. 103

In chapter 17, the seven heads and ten horns are on another beast, red like the dragon but bearing on its back another woman and this time not a mother but a harlot:

> I saw a woman sitting on a scarlet beast, full of blasphemous names, having seven heads and ten horns.
> (Rev 17:3)

These three creatures, the dragon and the two wild animals, have a great deal in common: they work together, they are ferocious, lethal enemies of God and His people, and they each have seven heads and ten horns.

As we will see, their 'blasphemous names' are claiming divine status.

Finally, after the third creature, John receives an explanation:

> And the angel said to me, 'Why do you wonder? I shall tell you the mystery of the woman and of the beast that carries her, which has the seven heads and the ten horns'
> (Rev 17:7)

For the purposes of this study, we will leave aside the identity of this woman and the two wild animals. What we need now is the meaning of the dragon and his seven heads:

> 'Here is the mind which has wisdom. The seven heads are seven mountains on which the woman sits, and they are seven kings; five have fallen, one is, the other has not yet come; and when he comes, he must remain a little while' (Rev 17:9-10)

Note there are two distinct symbolic meanings: 'the seven heads are seven mountains' and 'they are seven kings':

(i) The first metaphor, the 'seven mountains', is geographical. The woman or harlot is sitting at that time on Rome, the irresistible world power of the day, famous for being founded on seven hills or mountains.

(ii) The second metaphor, the 'seven kings', is historical and requires some knowledge of Jewish history; we would expect the first century church to have this, being founded by twelve Jewish apostles. The seven heads are 'seven kings' of whom 'five have fallen, one is', or exists at present, while the seventh is 'not yet come, and when he comes he must remain a little while.'

This interpretation given by the angel applies to all three occurrences of the seven heads.

As for the ten horns, down through the ages many have mistakenly assumed the horns were spread out as evenly as possible among the heads. Illustrious artists such as William Blake and Albrecht Dürer, for example, vividly imagined and painted these creatures and Blake's *The Great Red Dragon and the Beast from the Sea* (1805-10) has both figures with two horns on three of the heads and one horn on the other four; so too Dürer's *The Seven-Headed Dragon* (1496-98).

The angel, however, reveals that the time of the ten coming together is not until the last hour:

> 'The ten horns which you saw are ten kings who have not yet received a kingdom, but they receive authority as kings with the beast for one hour'(Rev 17:12)

They all therefore have to be on the seventh head.

Photo 2 — *The Revelation of St John: 10. The Woman Clothed With The Sun And The Seven-headed Dragon*, Albrecht Dürer (1471–1528)

'Seven Kings'

Some have tried to match the seven kings with the history of the Roman Empire, hoping these 'kings' might be successive Roman emperors, but there is no match. Domitian was already the eleventh when John was writing.

By 395 AD, when the Empire divided into East and West, there had been over a hundred and forty emperors. Besides, remember the point – the seven heads are on the dragon which is attacking the woman whom we know to be Israel. This vision is not to tell us about the Roman Empire but to reveal *the purpose of the history of Israel.*

In Jewish thinking, 'kings' and 'kingdom' can describe empires and dynasties (e.g. Dan 2:37-44, 5:31, 7:22-23) and from Israel's beginning until John's time, they had been successively ruled over by five great Gentile empires ('five have fallen') and were then under the domination of the sixth ('one is'). The five 'kings' were Egypt, Assyria, Babylon, Medo-Persia, and Greece, the sixth was Rome and the seventh was still in the future. Each is described in the Old Testament or foretold in Daniel so we will look at these soon.

So the seven heads show Satan's political machinations in response to God's creating a political entity of His own, the nation of Israel. The dragon is red, the colour of earth, because he is manifesting in the earth to oppose it. This vision is to reveal the common thread of Israel's first two thousand years: the *ever-recurring phenomenon* of anti-Semitic genocide and its demonic source. No matter that each of these Gentile kingdoms or empires grew from very different nations in very different localities and centuries apart – all were manipulated by Satan to attack the woman in order to destroy her child.

Everlasting Enmity

Why does the dragon murderously hate the woman and the child? Remember, John describes the great dragon as 'the serpent of old who is called the devil and Satan'. At the time he tempted Adam and Eve, God told him that a child of the woman would be his ultimate downfall:

> I will put enmity between you and the woman,
> And between your seed and her seed;
> He shall bruise you on the head,
> And you shall bruise Him on the heel (Gen 3:15)

The metaphor is astonishing. Picture a snake striking a man just as the man is treading on its head – both are 'bruised' or wounded, the snake biting the man's heel but notice where the man strikes the serpent. In Biblical typology, the head symbolises headship or government. So Satan knew from the very beginning, on the best possible authority, that one day the woman's child, Messiah, would trample on his 'head' or kingship, taking away his dominion over all the children of Adam and Eve.

No matter how big or glorious Satan's kingdom could ever become on earth, it will ultimately all be destroyed by the woman's child, Jesus, as His kingdom comes and 'the meek inherit the earth'. Notice too the weapons in this warfare – Satan uses the fabulously rich and powerful Gentile empires but God uses the power of love and sacrifice (2 Cor 10:3).

This is why the devil tempted Jesus in the wilderness with 'all the kingdoms of the world, and their glory', if only Jesus would fall down and worship him (Matt 4:8) – it was his last-ditch attempt to subvert the upcoming final battle of the ages. However, Satan was still promised the opportunity to wound Him 'on the heel', a concept later adapted into Greek mythology as Achilles' heel being the only place on his body where he was mortal and could be killed.

The crucifixion, then, was the serpent's striking the woman's Son on His heel, but also, without him realising it, the means of his own head being struck. As Paul explains:

> we speak God's wisdom in a mystery, the hidden wisdom which God predestined before the ages to our glory; the wisdom which none of the rulers of this age has understood for if they had understood it, they would not have crucified the Lord of glory (1 Cor 2:7-8)

We will return to this in some depth in my next book on Revelation chapter 13 where we will consider how exactly Satan was 'bruised' or wounded.

'Seven Diadems'

> 3. And another sign appeared in heaven: and behold, a great red dragon having seven heads and ten horns, and on his heads were seven diadems.

Here in Revelation 12, the diadems are on the dragon's seven heads whereas in Revelation 13, the diadems are on the beast's ten horns so there are ten diadems. In both instances, the Greek word used, *diadema*, is 'the symbol of kingly or imperial dignity'[14] and the angel tells John that both the heads and the horns are kings (Rev 17:10 & 12). This is to draw our attention in Revelation 12 to the kingdoms of the heads and in Revelation 13, to the kingdoms of the horns. Accordingly, we will leave the ten horns, their diadems and kingdoms until we study Chapter 13 and for now consider only the 'seven diadems' of the seven heads.

---

[14] See earlier reference at 'A crown of twelve stars'

(i) Egypt

The dragon's first diademed head, or Gentile kingdom, to reign over Israel was Egypt in the second millennium BC His attempt to devour the woman's child is seen in Pharaoh's command to kill all the male children in Israel (Ex 1:16 & 22). Moses was famously saved by his mother putting him in a basket in the reeds of the Nile where Pharaoh's daughter could find and adopt him. John's vision is therefore telling us what was going on behind the scenes in the spiritual realm: Pharaoh's attempt was motivated by much more than just his apparent fear of the Israelis becoming too numerous to be manageable. This massacre of the innocents was actually the first of Satan's political attempts to eradicate 'the seed of the woman'.

The prophet Isaiah clearly saw the work of the dragon in Egypt, writing almost seven hundred years later, in about 800 BC:

> Awake, awake, put on strength, O arm of the LORD;
> Awake as in the days of old, the generations of long ago.
> Was it not You who cut Rahab in pieces,
> Who pierced the dragon?
> Was it not You who dried up the sea,
> The waters of the great deep;
> Who made the depths of the sea a pathway
> For the redeemed to cross over? (Isa 51:9-10)

'Rahab' (Hebrew for 'boaster') was a Biblical nickname for Egypt (Isa 30:7, Psa 87:4) so Israel's exodus was God's intervention against both Egypt and Satan.

(ii) Assyria

The second head was the Assyrian empire. Due to a plague among their troops on the eve of the battle, as described in Lord Byron's well-known poem ('The Assyrian came down like the wolf on the fold... [but] melted like snow in the glance of the Lord'), the Assyrians were unable to defeat the tiny southern kingdom of Judah, but after conquering the much larger northern kingdom of Israel in 722 BC, they then tried to destroy them as a distinct people by assimilation. They moved many Israelis into other lands while moving other people-groups into the land of Israel (2 Kings 17:23-24). This was the origin of the Samaritans and why they were not accepted by the Jews of New Testament times. So we are being told to look behind the scenes again, to recognise that the Assyrian plan to assimilate Israel and destroy the nation as an identifiable entity is another attempt by Satan to destroy the woman and her child.

(iii) Babylonia

The third head was the Babylonians. They invaded the land of Israel and Judah, sacking Jerusalem and the Temple of Solomon in 586 BC. They then tried to assimilate Israel by taking the most outstanding Jewish youths back to Babylon where Daniel and his companions were tempted to forsake the food laws of Moses (Dan 1:8). When that failed, all of the Jewish exiles were tested through malicious men flattering the king into setting up the golden image (Dan 3:1ff): if the exiles could be forced to worship this image, they would lose their unique calling as a nation to bring forth Messiah; if they did not compromise, they would face annihilation as a people. We see then that the miraculous escape from the furnace by Shadrach, Meshach and Abed-nego saved not only them but their entire nation (Dan 3:28-29).

(iv) Medo-Persia

The fourth head was the Medo-Persian Empire. When the Medes and Persians defeated Babylon, they became the new captors of Israel. Esther records how the ambitious Haman, motivated by his hatred and jealousy of Mordecai, tried in

357 BC to destroy this godly man and the whole captive nation of Israel (Est 3:6). They were saved by the faith and courage of Esther who interceded with King Ahasuerus, but we need to appreciate that the threat she averted was the total extinction of the Jewish race. As hard as it may be to comprehend, Satan was able to use one man's hatred to bring the nation to the brink of extermination, to prevent the birth of Messiah.

Eventually, Cyrus the Persian emperor came to power and restored Israel to their land to rebuild Jerusalem and the temple. However, then came the fifth head.

(v) Greece

Under Alexander the Great, the Greeks were sympathetic towards Israel but after his death, his empire was divided into four and Israel came under the control of the infamous Antiochus Epiphanes. He tried to eradicate the Jewish faith, forbidding them to observe the Sabbath, the festivals, circumcision and the offering of their sacrifices. In 168 BC, he ordered all copies of the Law of Moses to be destroyed and desecrated the Temple in Jerusalem, dedicating it to Zeus and sacrificing a pig on the bronze altar (2 Macc 6:1-2). In 165 and 164 BC, he sent armies to exterminate the Jews as a people but Judas Maccabeus turned them back.

These then were the five kings that by John's time had fallen: Egypt, Assyria, Babylonia, Medo-Persia, and Greece.

(vi) Rome

The sixth head, described as 'one is' in John's time, is the Roman Empire. We come therefore to Herod's attempt to slay 'all the male children who were in Bethlehem and in all its environs, from two years old and under' (Matt 2:16). He had heard from the Magi of the birth of Messiah and, being unable to find Him, tried in this massacre of the innocents to destroy the Child.

The two millennia that lapsed between the first and the last of these acts of infanticide and attempted genocide can easily cause us to miss the connection so this vision was to reveal it: that behind all of these apparently isolated incidents in time and place is 'the dragon with the seven heads'. We also see confirmed the time-span of the vision so far: the time of the six heads extends from Israel's origin in Egypt to their Roman captivity.

The Seventh King

During the time of the sixth head, the nation of Israel lost not only the little boys of Bethlehem in about 4 BC; in 70 AD, as in the Babylonian exile, they lost almost everything when the Romans levelled the city of Jerusalem and the Temple. Over one million Jews died in this siege, and the survivors were enslaved or driven to the farthest corners of the earth. Thus began the longest exile of any nation in human history:

> 'But when you see Jerusalem surrounded by armies, then recognise that her desolation is near... for there will be great distress upon the land and wrath to this people; and they will fall by the edge of the sword, and will be led captive into all the nations; and Jerusalem will be trampled under foot by the Gentiles until the times of the Gentiles are fulfilled. (Luke 21:20 & 24)

Even in this scattering, or Diaspora, 'this people' were consistently targeted – in the Crusades of the 11th Century, the Spanish Inquisition of the 15th Century, in the 19th the Russian and Lithuanian pogroms and in the 20th, Hitler's attempted genocide. Compare Israel's history with that of any other nation. Benjamin Disraeli was once asked what proof there was of God's existence. He replied simply, 'Israel'. No other nation has so doggedly survived the many and blatant attempts to exterminate it, made by forces of overwhelming military superiority from their very beginning up to the present moment.

What then of the seventh head or king? Sadly, as if these persecutions and the Holocaust were not enough, we have yet to see the culmination of this vision with the seventh king, but see it we will. This head is significantly different from the other six in a way often overlooked as we saw earlier – it has the 'ten horns'. In Revelation 17, the angel gives this interpretation to John:

> And the ten horns which you saw are ten kings, who have not yet received a kingdom, but they receive authority as kings with the beast for one hour
> (Rev 17:12)

Notice the ten kings of the seventh kingdom only 'receive authority as kings... for one hour' and lose it all when Messiah comes to judge the earth (Rev 19:11-21). Accordingly, this kingdom can only come into full fruition 'one hour', or a very short time, before the Second Coming.

Notice too these ten 'receive authority as kings with the beast', when the seven-headed beast becomes resurgent. The meaning and timing of this coming Gentile kingdom of the ten horns and their ten diadems is beyond the scope of this book. We will leave that to be covered in the next book in this series which explores the vision of Revelation 13.

And what of Israel's response? Despite their long history as a nation of facing wave after wave of attempted genocide, their culture exalts in music and dance. Truly they are not just 'fiddlers on the roof' but, in Bruce Cockburn's memorable phrase, they are actually 'dancing in the dragon's jaws'.[15]

'A Third of the Stars'

We now come to consider a particular outcome of the dragon's attacks:

> And his tail swept away a third of the stars of heaven, and threw them to the earth. (Rev 12:4a)

Some teach from this verse that 'the stars of heaven' are angels as in Revelation 1:20, that one-third being swept away by the dragon's tail means that Satan, in his original rebellion against God, took with him a third of the angels. The corollary is that two-thirds of the angels, or twice as many, remain faithful to God and His people, which is a very comforting thought and a possible interpretation. There is no doubt that some angels followed Satan in his rebellion; verses 7 and 9 of this chapter refer to 'the dragon and his angels'. It appears too that God's angels outnumber the dragon's since Elisha could say, with regard to the angelic armies surrounding him and his servant:

> Do not fear, for those who are with us are more than those who are with them (2 Kings 6:16)

John's vision therefore could be referring to angels, but there are two problems with this interpretation. Firstly, these stars are 'swept away' and 'thrown to the earth' by the dragon's tail, rather than led or tempted away i.e. they have

---

[15] From Bruce Cockburn's 1979 album of the same title and used in his song *Hills of Morning*.

been forcibly overwhelmed by him. If these stars are indeed angels, how can God condemn them for 'abandoning their proper abode' (Jude 6) if they had no choice? Secondly, the timing of this event in Revelation 12:4 – Satan's leading astray of his angels was at the dawn of creation rather than during Israel's travails.

There is another interpretation which fits much more precisely. We have already seen that the twelve stars of Joseph's dream and this vision are the twelve sons of Israel rather than angels. We have seen God's repeated promise to Abraham and Isaac (see also Gen 22:17 and 26:4):

> And He took him outside and said, 'Now look toward the heavens, and count the stars, if you are able to count them.' And He said to him, 'So shall your descendants be' (Gen 15:5)

The 'stars of heaven' that the dragon 'sweeps away' and 'throws to the earth' are all the descendants of Abraham, Isaac and Jacob/Israel who have been killed in Satan's attacks throughout Jewish history.

As Jesus pointed out, when fishermen bring in their nets, they often catch 'by-catch' – unwanted fish which they throw away (Matt 13:47-48). Similarly in Satan's attempts to kill Messiah, many other Israelis were killed: when Moses was a new-born, many new-born baby boys of Israel were killed; literally millions of Israeli men, women and children died during the Assyrian, Babylonian, Greek, and Roman invasions and occupations as well as the 'massacre of the innocents' by Herod at the time of Jesus' birth. They were the dragon's by-catch or, in today's military euphemism, 'collateral damage'.

One third is not a precise number in Revelation's visions[16] and we have no way of establishing the exact numbers killed in any of these times.

However, there are some astonishing recent figures we can consider. On May 15, 1882, Tsar Alexander III decreed his infamous May Laws which openly aimed to force one third of Russia's Jews to emigrate, one third to convert to the Russian Orthodox faith and one third to perish by starvation.[17] In the Holocaust, an estimated 5,820,960 perished out of a world population of an estimated 16,648,000[18] which means about one third were put to death in World War II, a ratio also noted by Hannah Arendt in 1963.[19]

Accordingly, 'a third of the stars of heaven' being 'swept away' by the dragon's tail and 'thrown to the earth' are seen to be the many unfortunate children of Israel killed in Satan's continual attacks.

---

[16] For example, 'a third of the earth', 'a third of the trees' (Rev 8:7), 'a third of the sea' (v. 8), 'a third of the creatures' and 'a third of the ships' (v. 9), 'a third of the rivers and springs of water' (v. 10), 'a third of the sun and a third of the moon and a third of the stars' and 'the day not shining for a third of it' (v. 12)

[17] Elliot Rosenberg, *But Were They Good For the Jews? (Over 150 Historical Figures From A Jewish Perspective)*, New York; Birch Lane Press, 1997, p. 182

[18] http://faculty.ucc.edu/egh-damerow/Statistics.html, 27 Feb 2008. Today's population of Jews world-wide is estimated at 13 million by the *American Jewish Year Book, 2005*, www.us-israel.org/jsource/Judaism/jewpop.html, 11 Apr, 2007

[19] *Eichmann And The Holocaust*, Penguin Books, 2005, p. 90

3. Her Child

'Caught Up'

Returning now to the heart of the conflict:

> And the dragon stood before the woman who was about to give birth, so that when she gave birth he might devour her child.
> And she gave birth to a son, a male child, who is to rule all the nations with a rod of iron; and her child was caught up to God and to His throne. (Rev 12:4b-5)

The dragon stands there to 'devour her child' but John's vision makes no mention of any actual conflict, merely noting the outcome that the child 'was caught up to God and to His throne.' However, if we look at Jesus' earlier use of the same metaphor, we find many more details:

> 'for just as Jonah was three days and three nights in the belly of the sea monster, so shall the Son of Man be three days and three nights in the heart of the earth'
> (Matt 12:40)

There has been much debate about Jonah surviving three whole days inside a whale, the famous song from *Porgy and Bess* arguing that 'It Ain't Necessarily So', as if Jonah was only a good story. However the 'sea monster', or Leviathan, is another Biblical name for Satan:

> In that day the LORD will punish Leviathan the fleeing serpent,
> With His fierce and great and mighty sword,
> Even Leviathan the twisted serpent;
> And He will kill the dragon who lives in the sea (Isa 27:1)

In Biblical days, 'the sea' was also a symbol of 'the abyss' or bottomless pit, the place of the dead (Rom 10:7) and evil spirits (Luke 8:31, Rev 9:11). So, while Leviathan can be used to describe a whale (Psa 104:25-26), it 'ain't necessarily so' as it is also used to describe any large denizen of the deep, natural or spiritual, including the dragon.

There is also no Biblical insistence on Jonah remaining alive. He describes himself as going to the place of the dead (Jonah 2:2-6) but praying and repenting before he passed out (v. 7). It therefore seems more likely he was raised from the dead to fulfill the call of God which perfectly foreshadows Jesus' death and resurrection as well as the short-lived triumph of the dragon.

As for the 'three days and three nights', Jesus yielded to Judas's 'hour and the power of darkness' when He was arrested on the Thursday night (Luke 22:53), executed on the Friday (Matt 26:63-66), remained in the grave on the Saturday, only to be resurrected on the Sunday and given 'all authority in heaven and on earth':

> He humbled Himself by becoming obedient to the point of death, even death on a cross. Therefore God highly exalted Him, and bestowed on Him the name that is above every name, that at the name of Jesus every knee should bow, of those who are in heaven, and on earth, and under the earth, and that every tongue should confess that Jesus Christ is Lord, to the glory of God the Father (Phil 2:8-11)

Thus the woman's child is 'caught up to God and to His throne' and the dragon's initial success in devouring Him becomes the means of his ultimate undoing. Until He returns, Jesus rules as David prophesied:

> The LORD says to my Lord: 'Sit at My right hand,
> Until I make Your enemies a footstool for Your feet...
> Rule in the midst of Your enemies' (Psa 110:1-2)

The Father promised Him that His kingdom will only continue to grow until every enemy is defeated and indeed it has. It is often hard to get proper perspective from our Western media where Christians are usually only in the headlines because of traditional buildings becoming empty, paedophile priests, or immoral tele-evangelists. Globally, however, we are living in unprecedented times of Kingdom growth. The Chinese Government recently acknowledged that since 1948, when following Jesus became a criminal offence, His disciples have multiplied from about 1 million to 130 million, one tenth of the population! Best estimates have Latin America's disciples at almost 520 million, Africa 400 million and in Asia, India alone has recently climbed to 70 million. Most sources, including the BBC, *Encyclopedia Britannica* and Wikipedia, show professing Christians numbering some 2 billion or a third of the earth's population.[20]

'And the Woman Fled'

> And the woman fled into the wilderness... (Rev 12:6a)

Returning to first century Israel, was this to be their end? Messiah had come as promised but 'those who were His own did not receive Him' (John 1:11), demanding instead that the Romans put Him to death. Forty year later, in 70 AD, Titus and the legions sacked Jerusalem and the

---

[20] www.religioustolerance.org/worldrel.htm, 3 Dec, 2007

magnificent Temple, killing over a million Jews and leading almost a hundred thousand survivors into slavery and exile. Israel was no longer a sovereign nation, just as Jesus had predicted:

> Truly I say to you, all these things shall come upon this generation.
> Jerusalem, Jerusalem, who kills the prophets and stones those who are sent to her! How often I wanted to gather your children together, the way a hen gathers her chicks under her wings, and you were unwilling. Behold, your house is being left to you desolate! (Matt 23:36-38)

Was God giving up on Israel? Sadly, many Christians through the ages have believed so, assuming that God had rejected Israel and replaced her with the Church. Of course Israel did lose Jerusalem, the land and the temple for the second time. Of course the church, comprising both Jewish and Gentile believers, did gain the new and better covenant, but God no more gave up on Israel than He did when they were in exile for the first time, in Babylon.

All of us who are Gentiles need to be acutely aware that misunderstanding this has led directly to some of the most appalling tragedies in human history, including the Holocaust. Hitler reaped his harvest of murderous anti-Semitism from centuries of seeds sown in Europe, some by one of the most famous men in Christian history, Martin Luther. Rightly revered amongst Protestants for restoring 'justification by faith' early in the sixteenth century, Luther also taught two heresies – hatred of the Jewish people and undue submission by believers to secular authorities. In *The Rise and Fall of the Third Reich*, William Shirer comments:

It is difficult to understand the behaviour of most German Protestants in the first Nazi years unless one is aware of two things: their history and the influence of Martin Luther. The great founder of Protestantism was both a passionate anti-Semite and a ferocious believer in absolute obedience to political authority. He wanted Germany rid of the Jews and when they were sent away he advised that they be deprived of 'all their cash and jewels and silver and gold' and, furthermore, 'that their synagogues or schools be set on fire, that their houses be broken up and destroyed… and they be put under a roof or stable, like the gypsies… in misery and captivity as they incessantly lament and complain to God about us' – advice that was literally followed four centuries later by Hitler, Goering and Himmler.[21]

Luther had earlier, in 1519, recognised and denounced anti-Semitism:

> Absurd theologians defend hatred for the Jews. … What Jew would consent to enter our ranks when he sees the cruelty and enmity we wreak on them – that in our behaviour towards them we less resemble Christians than beasts?[22]

In 1523, he wrote in *That Jesus Christ Was Born a Jew:*

> Our fools, the popes, bishops, sophists, and monks – the crude asses' heads – have hitherto so treated the Jews that anyone who wished to be a good Christian

---

[21] P. 236. Shirer is quoting Luther's infamous essay, '*The Jews And Their Lies*' (1543) and referring to *Luther Against The Peasants* (1525)

[22] Luther was arguing against *Servitus Judaeorum (Servitude of the Jews)*, published as a law in 529 AD by the emperor Justinian I in *Corpus Juris Civilis*. Quoted by Elliot Rosenberg, *But Were They Good for the Jews?* New York; Birch Lane Press, 1997, p. 65

would almost have had to become a Jew. If I had been a Jew and had seen such dolts and blockheads govern and teach the Christian faith, I would sooner have become a hog than a Christian.

They have dealt with the Jews as if they were dogs rather than human beings; they have done little else than deride them and seize their property…

If the apostles, who also were Jews, had dealt with us Gentiles as we Gentiles deal with the Jews, there would never have been a Christian among the Gentiles. Since they dealt with us Gentiles in such brotherly fashion, we in our turn ought to treat the Jews in a brotherly manner…

When we are inclined to boast of our position we should remember that we are but Gentiles, while the Jews are of the lineage of Christ. We are aliens and in-laws; they are blood relatives, cousins, and brothers of our Lord. Therefore, if one is to boast of flesh and blood, the Jews are actually nearer to Christ than we are, as St. Paul says in Romans 9[:5].[23]

Tragically, by 1543 he had abandoned this revelation of the Jews and published *On the Jews and Their Lies*, as quoted by Shirer above. Just like the apostle Peter, and every single one of us, he could receive divine revelation at one moment but be used by Satan the next (Matt 16:17 cf. 16:23). Shirer therefore argues that for all the good Luther did in reforming the church, he also polluted it by being 'both a passionate anti-Semite and a ferocious believer in absolute obedience to political authority'.

---

[23] http://www.ccjr.us/dialogika-resources/primary-texts-from-the-history-of-the-relationship/272-luther-1523, 8 June, 2010.

As a direct consequence, the Lutheran Church as the national church of Germany was slow and subdued in their opposition to the Nazis' unmitigated evil.

However, the Lutherans were not the only denomination to be misled. From at least the fourth century, both the Eastern Orthodox and the western Roman Catholic churches employed the pejorative 'Christ-killers' to justify the plunder and murder of Jews, the worst instances being the Catholic Crusades from the 11th to the 14th Centuries, their 15th Century Inquisition, and the Orthodox churches' pogroms in eastern Europe in the 19th Century. It was not until the Second Vatican Council (1962-65) that the Roman Catholic Church finally renounced anti-Semitism (*Nostra Aetate*, 'In Our Time', October 28, 1965), leaving it until 1999 before Pope John Paul II officially apologised to Israel for their part in the terrible injustices.

The appalling tragedy of God's people acting in His name while actually assisting the dragon to 'throw to the earth' so many children of Israel is not to be glossed over. Such heresies were only possible because we departed from the plain teachings and clear warnings of the Scriptures:

> I say then, God has not rejected His people, has He? May it never be! (Rom 11:1)

> I say then, they did not stumble so as to fall, did they? May it never be! (Rom 11:11)

> From the standpoint of the gospel they are enemies for your sake, but from the standpoint of God's choice they are beloved for the sake of the fathers; for the gifts and the calling of God are irrevocable (Rom 11:28-29)

Paul is unequivocal – even as unbelieving enemies of the gospel, they remain beloved by God.

Paul plainly warned us that even though many Jews were 'branches broken off' the olive tree because of their unbelief, we were to be careful of our attitude towards every one of them:

Do not be arrogant towards the branches (Rom 11:17)

Sadly, many today still believe the New Testament is anti-Semitic. As if it could be, written almost entirely by Jews and, as we can see in this vision of John's, actually revealing that anti-Semitism is demonically inspired.

So, if God did not give up on Israel, what was supposed to happen to them after they rejected Jesus?

'A Place Prepared by God'

And the woman fled into the wilderness where she had a place prepared by God, so that there she might be nourished for one thousand, two hundred and sixty days (Rev 12:6)

It is essential we understand God's attitude towards Israel: He had 'a place prepared' for her but it is in the wilderness. Many years earlier, when God had first wanted Israel to enter the Promised Land, they refused so His response was to lead them back into the wilderness for forty years (Num 14:26-35). This time, their refusal takes them back into the wilderness where they will be 'nourished' or sustained for 1,260 days which, when divided by thirty (the lunar month and standard Jewish measure in those days), is exactly forty two months or three and a half years.

This sojourn in the wilderness is described in more detail in verses 13-17 so we will leave our consideration of it until then. Suffice it to say for now that God did not give up on

Israel, despite their rejection of Messiah. He still had plans for her when John was writing Revelation in about 100 AD and He has plans for her still, as we will see. As for this specific time period, it twice appears in Daniel (7:25, 12:7) and four more times in Revelation (11:2-3, 12:6 & 14, 13:5), being in itself a mystery which we will need to closely examine.

Summary

To summarise what we have established so far:

> (i) The woman is revealed to be the nation of Israel by each of three identifying features – being clothed with the sun, with the moon at her feet and crowned with twelve stars. These came from Joseph's dream which occurred at the very beginning of Israel's growing from a family to a nation.

> (ii) Unique among the nations on earth, this woman, the nation of Israel, exists to give birth to Messiah.

> (iii) The dragon, symbolising Satan, tried to prevent that. His seven heads are seen to be seven Gentile empires, five of which had by the first century AD already ruled over Israel – Egypt, Assyria, Babylon, Medo-Persia and Greece. The sixth, Rome, was in John's time ruling over Israel and the seventh was yet to come.

> (iv) The dragon is red, the colour of the earth, because he is manifest in the earth in the apparently random attacks by each of these empires on the woman and her children over the preceding two thousand years.

(v) Satan's casting down of 'a third of the stars of heaven' is the killing of many of the descendants of Abraham, Isaac, and Jacob/Israel.

(vi) The child is Jesus 'who is to rule all nations with a rod of iron' but first is 'caught up to God and to His throne'. This is His resurrection from the dead and ascension to the throne, where He is waiting until all His enemies are made 'a footstool for His feet'.

(vii) In the meantime, the woman is forced to flee into the wilderness for 'one thousand, two hundred and sixty days', the mysterious three and a half year time period that will be examined in Chapter 6.

(viii) The dragon's seventh head has ten horns and these will be explained in the next book in this series which considers Revelation 13.

4. The Ruler of the World

Israel at the Time of Jesus

John's vision then shifts back into the heavens:

> 7. And there was war in heaven, Michael and his angels waging war with the dragon. And the dragon and his angels waged war,
> 8. and they were not strong enough, and there was no longer a place found for them in heaven.
> 9. And the great dragon was thrown down, the serpent of old who is called the devil and Satan, who deceives the whole world; he was thrown down to the earth, and his angels were thrown down with him.
> 10. And I heard a loud voice in heaven, saying: 'Now the salvation, and the power, and the kingdom of our God and the authority of His Christ have come, for the accuser of our brethren has been thrown down, who accuses them before our God day and night' (Rev 12:7-10)

'The Great Dragon Was Thrown Down'

This passage describes the epoch-changing heavenly effects, early in the first century AD, of Jesus of Nazareth coming into His kingdom as He 'bruised the head' of Satan. There are several ways of establishing this timing. Firstly, Jesus told us after His resurrection:

> All authority has been given to Me in heaven and on earth (Matt 28:18).

Secondly, just before His crucifixion Jesus gave a specific time when Satan would be 'cast out':

And so 'the great dragon was thrown down'. This spiritual battle being fought by 'Michael and his angels' confirms yet again the identity of the woman because he is 'the great prince who stands guard over the sons of Israel' (Dan 12:1). As the great guardian angel of the whole nation of Israel, Michael leads the fight in the heavenly realm when the woman finally brings forth the Child to deal with all the sin of mankind.

We also see 'the accuser of our brethren has been thrown down' (v. 10). The Greek word translated as accuser is *kategor* and its nearest equivalent today is the prosecutor or prosecuting attorney in our law courts. He is completely silenced in the case of everyone who has accepted both their guilt and God's forgiveness through Jesus' death and resurrection (Rom 10:9-10).

The Believers' Part in This Warfare

Now John goes on to reveal the Christians' part in this spiritual warfare. He hears the voice describing the believers of his day as overcoming Satan, even though they were still dying in the circuses of Rome or at the hands of Caesar's magistrates for their refusal to worship Caesar:

> And they [the brethren] overcame him [the dragon] because of the blood of the Lamb and because of the word of their testimony, and they did not love their life even to death (Rev 12:11)

In other words, these believers are martyrs. Today's English word 'martyr' is simply a transliteration of the

Greek noun *martus* which means a witness or someone who gives testimony in a court of law.

John had actually seen these martyrs earlier, at the opening of the fifth seal. He was told then they were slain 'because of the testimony which they had maintained' but also to wait 'until the number of their fellow servants and their brethren who were to be killed even as they had been, would be completed also' (Rev 6:9-11). This number will not be completed until Jesus returns and halts all need for this kind of testimony.

It has been widely overlooked by Western media but in the Sudan alone, between 1985 and 2007, well over one million Christians were martyred by the Islamic government of Omar al-Bashir.[24]

We still have to wage war to overcome Satan on earth and we too have been handed these three irresistible spiritual weapons: 'the blood of the Lamb', 'the word of (our) testimony' and 'not loving (our) lives even to death.' Much needs to be said about these but that is outside the scope of this study so for now, if we want to overcome the dragon in our own lives, we have to trust in 'the blood' (i.e. Jesus' death on the cross for our sins), to speak openly or testify to our faith in Him, and lastly, to be willing to die at the hands of His enemies.

---

[24] http://satucket.com/lectionary/Sudan.htm, 22 June, 2009. This averaged out as one hundred and twenty five a day!

'Rejoice O Heavens'

> For this reason, rejoice O heavens and you who dwell in
> them. Woe to the earth and the sea, because the devil
> has come down to you, having great wrath, knowing
> that he has only a short time (Rev 12:12)

We who are 'citizens of heaven' (Phil 3:20) can rejoice in the devil's downfall; in stark contrast, the citizens of this world are still 'in the power of the evil one' (1 John 5:19, Eph 2:2) as we can readily see every day in the news headlines. They can also still be validly accused by him.

As for 'the earth and the sea', reading on to Revelation 13, we see the devil's 'great wrath' is outworked through two huge wild beasts, the first emerging from the sea (Rev 13:1) and the second from the earth (Rev 13:11). Again, we have to leave these to be examined in the next study.

In the meantime, the good news is that, from the perspective of eternity, 'he has only a short time' left (v. 12). During this time, Satan ('the ruler of this world') is 'cast out' of the lives of all of us who are no longer 'of this world' and he is 'thrown down' from heaven to the earth, in that he can no longer accuse any believers before the Father, as he could Job (Job 1:6-11). We can rejoice in our deliverance.

Summary

(i) Satan and his angels are cast out from the presence of God by Michael and his angels because 'there was no longer a place found for them in heaven.'

(ii) Michael's role further confirms the woman as Israel because he is the archangel who guards that nation.

(iii) Satan can no longer justly accuse any who are trusting for forgiveness in the death, resurrection and ascension of Jesus, Israel's Messiah. 'The blood of the Lamb' has cleansed them from all sin so by their testimony and their commitment they can now overcome Satan as their accuser.

5. Into the Wilderness

Israel After Jesus

And when the dragon saw that he was thrown down to the earth, he persecuted the woman who gave birth to the male child. And the two wings of the great eagle were given to the woman, in order that she might fly into the wilderness... (Rev 12:13-14)

In verse 5, we saw in the birth of the Child the beginning of a very new era. Accordingly, the Gregorian calendar, the most common in use today, bisects recorded history into BC (Before Christ) and AD (*Anno Domine*, lit. year of the Lord). This constant acknowledgement of Jesus offends some secular and religious sensibilities so they prefer to speak of BCE (Before Common Era) and CE (Common Era). The Jewish calendar, on the other hand, dates everything from an ancient estimate of the creation of Adam so 2000 AD was their year 5760.

In John's vision, the history of Israel is obviously in the two eras and we saw the first in Chapter 1. Revelation 12:1-6 covers the first two thousand years, from the nation's beginning as an extended family in Egypt in the eighteenth century BC through to the first century AD and the coming of Jesus as Messiah. Then in the last chapter regarding Revelation 12:7-12, we looked briefly at the heavenly consequences at that time, when Satan was cast down.

Now we come to consider, in verses 13-17, the earthly consequences and the second era of Israel's history. This will cover, firstly, from 30 AD to the present day, when they are back in the land, and then on to their projected future.

Who Exactly *Is* Israel Today?

It may seem odd to ask who is Israel today, given there is a whole nation in the Middle East by that name, but put it another way: 'Who or what exactly is a Jew?' Up until 1st Century AD, all it took was a genealogical check. Originally, a Jew was a citizen of the southern kingdom of Judah which was divided from the northern kingdom of Israel in 10th Century BC (1 Kings 12) but four hundred years later the two kingdoms were reunited in the Babylonian exile (Ezek 37:15-22) so, by 1st Century AD, 'Jew' had become interchangeable with 'Israelite' (today's 'Israeli') and 'Hebrew' (e.g. Rom 11:1, Phil 3:5).

These terms therefore described any descendant of Abraham, Isaac, and Jacob/Israel through the male line e.g. Moses married a Gentile (or non-Jew) yet his children were considered Jewish, as was David whose grandmother was a Gentile, Ruth. Also included were any who converted to the Jewish faith. However, in the time of Nehemiah in 5th Century BC, intermarriage became so common as to overwhelm their Jewish identity so he called for Jews to marry only Jews (Neh 13:23ff).

All the genealogical records were burned with the Temple in 70 AD and being Jewish came to be defined through the female line or conversion:

> A Jew is any person whose mother was a Jew or any person who has gone through the formal process of conversion to Judaism. It is important to note that being a Jew has nothing to do with what you believe or what you do. A person born to non-Jewish parents who has not undergone the formal process of conversion but who believes everything that Orthodox Jews believe and observes every law and custom of Judaism is still a non-Jew, even in the eyes of the most liberal

movements of Judaism, and a person born to a Jewish mother who is an atheist and never practices the Jewish religion is still a Jew, even in the eyes of the ultra-Orthodox. In this sense, Judaism is more like a nationality than like other religions, and being Jewish is like a citizenship.[25]

This is no small matter. Israel's attempts in recent years to define Israeli citizenship and national boundaries to prevent their being outnumbered, and therefore out-voted, by the Palestinian Arabs have many times incurred the wrath of the United Nations. Condemned as racist if they proceed but overwhelmed if they do not, Israel's situation remains, as always, precarious.

The most commonly held Christian view of Israel is a 'spiritualising' of it i.e. that in the first century, everything God promised to Israel was transferred to the church or what some call 'spiritual Israel'. This is called *Supersessionism* (from to supersede – to cause to be set aside, to take the place or position of another) or Replacement Theology. Until 1965, this was the official teaching of the Roman Catholic Church[26] with about one billion adherents. It is also taught in Reformed covenant

---

[25] Judaism 101 website, http://www.jewfaq.org/whoisjew.htm, 16 Apr, 2007

[26] 'Supersessionism dates from the second century and holds that Jews have lost any right to the Land of Israel because their status as God's people has been superseded by the Christian Church… Catholic attitudes have been dominated by supersessionism (but) beginning with the 1965 Second Vatican Council declaration, *Nostra Aetate*, the Catholic magisterium (teaching authority) has repudiated supersessionism and affirmed repeatedly that God's covenant with the Jewish people endures', Phillip A Cunningham, Reflections from a Roman Catholic on 'Understanding Christian Support for Israel' http://www.bc.edu/research/cjl/meta-elements/texts/cjrelations/resources/articles/cunningham_14Mar07.htm, 16 Apr, 2007

theology.[27] It is also, as might be expected, the most popular view amongst Palestinian Christians and is the basis of their claim that Israel has no Biblical right to the land.

So, which is true? Is Israel a physical or genetic reality, consisting of all the descendants of Abraham, Isaac, and Jacob/Israel, regardless of their faith or lack of it? Or has God replaced it with the church? In true Jewish fashion, the answers are both yes and no! For full details, see Appendix A: *Which Israel?*

The Earthly and the Heavenly

It is an easy but very big mistake to make, to believe that the spiritual replaced the natural, as if it had to be 'either/or'. We need to recognise that when God made His covenant with Abraham, He specifically promised him many descendants of both kinds. When he first arrived in Canaan, the Lord told him:

> 'For all the land which you see, I will give it to you and to your descendants forever. I will make your descendants as the dust of the earth, so that if anyone can number the dust of the earth, then your descendants can also be numbered' (Gen 13:15-16)

Some time later, the Lord used a second analogy:

> 'Now look toward the heavens, and count the stars, if you are able to count them.' And He said to him, 'So shall your descendants be.' (Gen 15:5)

This promise of the stars was repeated to Isaac (Gen 26:4) and illustrated in Joseph's dream (Gen 37:9). However, in

---

[27] R Todd Mangum, '*A Future For Israel In Covenant Theology; The Untold Story*' http://www.biblical.edu/images/connect/PDFs/A %20Future%20for%20Israel.pdf, 12 May, 2008

speaking to Abraham, the Lord also used a third analogy, this time of grains of sand:

> 'I will greatly multiply your descendants like the stars of the heavens, and as the sand which is on the seashore...' (Gen 22:17)

Notice there are two kinds of descendants – one of the earth and the other of the heavens. God does not tell Abraham they will be like either the stars or the dust and sand. He says 'and'. Today, these promises of dust or sand and stars are still being fulfilled, in natural and spiritual Israel.

The Fig Tree and the Olive Tree

Another picture of this in the Scriptures can be seen in two trees, the fig and the olive. These illustrate that the two very different entities named 'Israel' have not only very different compositions but very different destinies and therefore two different paths through time in God's purposes.

In about 500 BC, Jeremiah was given a vision concerning Israel in which the Lord describes His people as two kinds of figs:

> Behold, two baskets of figs before the temple of the Lord!
> One basket had very good figs, like first-ripe figs; and the other basket had very bad figs, which could not be eaten due to rottenness (Jer 24:1-3)

The Lord then explains the parable for Jeremiah, that these are two kinds of Israelis. The first, obedient to the word of the Lord by surrendering to the Babylonians (Jer 27:8-17), God would preserve as 'very good' figs but those who were disobedient, He would 'abandon' as 'very bad', inedible, rotten figs (Jer 24:8).

All of these figs are produced by the fig tree which symbolises the 'natural' nation of Israel (Joel 1:6-7) and is comprised of all the natural descendants of Abraham, Isaac and Jacob over all generations, both those who have faith and those who do not.

Earlier, Hosea had prophesied similarly:

> I found Israel like grapes in the wilderness;
> I saw your forefathers as the earliest fruit on the fig tree
> in its first season.
> But they came to Baal-peor and devoted themselves to
> shame,
> And they became as detestable as that which they loved
> (Hos 9:10)

Just as God delighted in Israel during the Exodus as 'grapes in the wilderness' and 'the earliest fruit on the fig tree in its first season' only to find they became shameless and 'detestable', so Jeremiah predicted the nation's exile because they were still unwilling to bear the right fruit:

> 'I will surely snatch them away [into Babylon],' declares
> the LORD;
> 'There will be no grapes on the vine
> And no figs on the fig tree,
> And the leaf will wither;
> And what I have given them will pass away' (Jer 8:13)

Notice God's resignation that there will be 'no figs on the fig tree', that 'the leaf will wither' and that all He gave Israel will be lost. This enables us to now put into proper context both a parable Jesus taught and an apparently bizarre display of power:

Here Jesus uses the normal, legitimate impatience any owner has with persistently unfruitful trees to illustrate God's impatience with Israel after three years of Messiah's ministry. Just as the vineyard-keeper interceded for another year of grace, Jesus laying down even His own life in the fourth year had given the fig tree every possible opportunity to bear fruit.

In the days immediately preceding His death, as He entered Jerusalem Jesus predicted the aftermath of this fruitlessness with a graphic demonstration:

Despite the fig tree fruiting for some ten months of the year in the Middle East, Mark specifically records that it was 'not the season for figs.' Since Jesus would have known the season as well as the disciples did, His unexpected and apparently unreasonable response to this particular tree obviously intrigued them. They kept listening for another, deeper significance which Jesus provided soon after:

> As they were passing by in the morning, they saw the fig tree withered from the roots up. And being reminded, Peter said to Him, 'Rabbi, behold, the fig tree which You cursed has withered.' Jesus answered, saying to them, 'Have faith in God' (Mark 11:20-22)

This fig tree's demise powerfully demonstrated the direct consequences to the nation of Israel of their failure to have faith. As Paul wrote, they became 'accursed' and 'separated from Christ' and within one generation in 70 AD, they completely withered as a nation. As the tree withered 'from the roots up', so Israel was to lose their land at that time.

To further clarify, Jesus then gave the disciples another parable about a vineyard – because Israel was refusing to give God the fruit He rightly expected, mistreating and killing His prophets and even His Son, God would 'destroy the vine-growers and give the vineyard to others' (Mark 12:1-12).

Later when the disciples asked when He would come in His kingdom, Jesus replied:

> Now learn the parable from the fig tree: when its branch has already become tender, and puts forth its leaves, you know the summer is near.
> Even so, you too, when you see these things happening, recognise that He is near, right at the door (Mark 13:28-29)

We see then that the fig tree illustrates the natural nation of Israel, regardless of the faith or otherwise of individuals within it, and that simply belonging to that nation is no guarantee of salvation. Only good figs, i.e. those trusting in His word, are acceptable to God. We also need to keep our eyes on the fig tree to see if 'summer is near'.

The Olive Tree

Jeremiah also gives us the metaphor of the olive tree when he prophesies to Israel:

> The LORD called your name, 'A green olive tree, beautiful in fruit and form';
> With the noise of a great tumult He has kindled fire on it,
> And its branches are worthless.
> And the LORD of hosts, who planted you, has pronounced evil against you because of the evil of the house of Israel and of the house of Judah, which they have done to provoke Me by offering sacrifices to Baal (Jer 11:16-17)

The olive tree is 'the house of Israel' and 'the house of Judah' together, the twin kingdoms that made up the whole nation of Israel in Jeremiah's day. God removed the 'worthless' branches, i.e. individual Jews/Israelis, for their unfaithfulness to Him.

Six hundred years later, Paul uses Jeremiah's metaphor to teach Gentiles the ways of God:

> But if some of the branches were broken off, and you [Gentiles], being a wild olive, were grafted in among them [Jewish believers] and became partaker with them of the rich root of the olive tree, do not be arrogant toward the branches; but if you are arrogant, remember that it is not you who supports the root, but the root supports you (Rom 11:17-18)

The olive tree is 'spiritual' Israel, olive oil being a symbol of the Holy Spirit. This tree does not 'wither from the roots up' – it cannot, because it began with Abraham, Isaac and Jacob who were faithful to the end – but instead it is only pruned of unbelieving 'branches', their descendants who did not remain faithful:

> …they were broken off for their unbelief, but you stand by your faith. Do not be conceited but fear; for if God did not spare the natural branches, neither will He spare you (Rom 11:20)

Only those who remain faithful can be 'partakers of the rich root of the olive tree' (v. 17).

The Fig, the Olive and the Land

God wants healthy fruit from both trees and in both cases, the fruit is faith – whole-hearted trust in Him and in His words. We can however contrast the two trees as follows:

> (i) The fig tree symbolises the nation of Israel in the land of Israel. Its withering and dying, then budding and bearing fruit, illustrates the demise and resurrection of the nation of Israel in the land of Israel. No-one is saved by belonging to the fig tree.

> (ii) The olive tree is the people of Israel, being portrayed as losing or gaining branches. Jewish branches becoming unfaithful are 'broken off', while branches from 'wild olives' (i.e. Gentiles who have become faithful) are 'grafted in'. Everyone is saved by belonging to the olive tree.

> (iii) The fig tree's capital city is 'natural' or old Jerusalem (Rev 11:2), while the olive tree's is 'the

heavenly Jerusalem' (Heb 12:22) or 'new Jerusalem' (Rev 21:2).

(iv) While the olive tree is pruned as often as necessary, the fig tree needed a resurrection.

Summary of the Two Israels

Revelation 12:13-14 begins with the woman being chased into the wilderness and since she, up until now, has been the whole nation of Israel, we need to establish why. First, however, we needed to recognise that at this point, the Scripture began to refer to two distinct entities called 'Israel'. This is because in the first century, many in Israel were faithful and accepted Jesus as their Messiah but many did not, thus separating the nation into two entities, illustrated by several metaphors:

> (i) Abraham's descendants as the dust or sand (i.e. of the earth and 'natural'), and as the stars (i.e. of the heavens and 'spiritual').

> (ii) the fig tree (i.e. 'natural Israel' in the land), and the olive tree (i.e. 'spiritual Israel' anywhere).

In considering the woman in the wilderness, we will therefore see the outcome for natural Israel, the literal descendants of Abraham, who were driven out of the land in 70 AD Later, we will also see the outcome for spiritual Israel.

Israel's Unique Gifts and Calling

Some object to the nation Israel continuing to have a special identity or unique calling today. However, Paul is explicit:

Some argue today that God can only have one people at a time, first Israel but now the church. However, Paul reveals here that God has two peoples, the church and Israel, albeit with different destinies as seen in the olive tree and the fig tree, but he is explicit – even in their rejection of Messiah, as 'enemies' of the gospel, the Jewish people remain 'beloved' by God, not for their own sake but 'for the sake of the fathers.' God's gifts and calling of the Jews will simply never be withdrawn.

Jeremiah confirms this:

Note, this calling is despite 'all that they have done' (v. 37).

But what exactly are 'the gifts and the calling of God', unique to Israel, which are 'irrevocable' or unalterable? Since God has called all men everywhere to repent and be saved

---

(Acts 17:30, 2 Pet 3:9), that calling is not unique to Israel; God so loves the whole world that He gave us His Son (John 3:16), so the gift of His Son is not only for Israel; He gives natural gifts and talents to everyone (Acts 14:16-17) so neither are these unique to Israel; He promises the Holy Spirit and the spiritual gifts to as many as are willing to accept them (Acts 2:38-39, 1 Cor 14:1), so these are not unique to Israel.

So what 'gifts and calling' are unique to Israel? Their history, the Old Testament Scriptures, the covenants and the patriarchs were *initially* unique to Israel (Rom 3:1-2, 9:4-5). Some therefore argue today that since Paul does not include the land here, he meant that Israel has forever lost it. However, Paul is actually explaining the advantage Israel received from having first access to these gifts to which we who are Gentiles later received access as well: Israel's history (1 Cor 10:1-11), the Scriptures (Rom 15:4), covenants (Eph 2:12) and patriarchs (Rom 4:16-17, 11:17-24). Accordingly, since we were not at any time promised the land, Paul should not have included it in these passages.

On the other hand, the people of Israel were uniquely promised the land (Gen 13:15-16)[28] and 'the beloved city', Jerusalem (Psa 48:1-2, Zech 12:1-2, Luke 21:24, Rev 20:9). These were, are, and will always remain unique gifts to the physical descendants of Abraham, Isaac and Jacob as long as

---

[28] See also Gen 12:7, 15:7 & 18, 17:8; Psa 105:11, 135:12; Isa 14:1-2; Jer 7:7, 16:15, 25:5; Ezek 20:39-44, 37:25; 38:8-23, 39:25-28, 47:13-23; Dan 9:2 & 19; Joel 3:1-2; Amos 9:14-15; Zech 2:12, 12:2

this earth exists. Israel's unique calling is to inhabit this land when God allows them (Zech 12:1-3, 10).[29]

However, it is not as if God is showing undue favouritism because He has also given every other nation on the earth a portion of land:

> ...and He made from one (Adam), every nation of mankind to live on all the face of the earth, having determined their appointed times, and the boundaries of their habitation (Acts 17:26)

He gave the land of China to the Chinese, Korea to the Koreans, Fiji to the Fijians and the vast majority of the Middle East to the Arabs. While we argue over borders or immigration, every people group has a homeland and every land has indigenous people because God has 'determined their appointed times' as well as 'the boundaries' of 'every nation of mankind'. We therefore have to humble ourselves to learn from Him where and when He has decided every

---

[29] This condition of when God allows is often misunderstood. For example, some teach that the Jews will only be legitimately in the land when they have faith, noting that most in Israel today are decidedly unbelieving. However, Ezekiel 36:8-36 is explicit – God restored the people to the land from Babylon while they were still in unbelief. Conversely, He warned them when they were about to lose their land for seventy years (Jer 25:1-11). This was when many were believing that He would not allow such a calamity (Jer 23:17). However, He promised their restoration in His timing (Jer 29:10 cf. Dan 9:2 & 25). Similarly, Jesus warned that Israel would lose the land, then regain it after 'the times of the Gentiles' (Luke 21:20-24). We need to pay close attention to this very important prophecy because many today are overlooking the word and work of God in fulfilling His promises to Israel in 1948 and 1967. It is also an identifying characteristic of the spirit of antichrist to try to drive Israel out again at the end of this age (Rev 16:13-16, 20:7-9).

nation should be, including present-day Jews and Palestinians. This is no easy task because the world has never sought to cooperate with Him.

Today, Israel consists of five-and-a-half million Jews and two million non-Jews living in 8,000 square miles of land. Its very existence is deeply resented by the surrounding Arab nations, also descendants of Abraham through Ishmael and Esau but numbering around 320 million people, in twenty two countries and 5.25 million square miles. This area is one and a half times the size of the United States of America. Saudi Arabia's land alone is over one hundred times greater than Israel's, and includes almost a quarter of the world's known oil reserves. The Jewish people have often been quite rueful about this: 'If only Moses had turned right instead of left!' Sadly, the irrational resentment of Israel's existence in their own land is openly justified by the increasingly wide-spread teachings of fundamentalist Islam, as will be considered in the next book in this series.

Of course, we also need to consider the very painful issues for the Palestinian Arabs affected today by Israel's restoration (see Appendices D, E and F). In the meantime, returning to Revelation 12, we find further evidence that God did not finish with the fig tree, the nation of Israel, in 70 AD.

The New Era's Time-Span

We have to carefully establish this time span because of many strongly competing assertions. Some Christian theologians teach, for example, that this time period was all over by 70 AD with the destruction of Jerusalem.[30] Others argue it

---

[30] For example, David Chilton, *The Days of Vengeance - An Exposition of the Book of Revelation,* Fort Worth; Dominion Press, 1990.

has not yet begun, and indeed cannot, until the final Antichrist appears and makes a covenant with Israel. This view has been popularised in Tim LaHaye and Jerry Jenkins' *Left Behind* series, sixteen books published between 1995 and 2007 which have sold over sixty five million copies and adapted into feature films, a children's series and graphic novels. Somewhere in the middle, the Jehovah's Witnesses claim this period ended in 1914.

So, returning to Revelation 12, we need to recognise that with Messiah caught up to God, the woman begins a new era fleeing for a particular time period:

> …and her child was caught up to God and to His throne. Then the woman fled into the wilderness where she had a place prepared by God, so that there she might be nourished for one thousand, two hundred and sixty days. (Rev 12:5-6)

We saw earlier, in lunar measurement this is exactly three and a half years. Again in verse 14:

> And the two wings of a great eagle were given to the woman, in order that she might fly into the wilderness to her place, where she was nourished for a time and times and half a time, from the presence of the serpent (Rev 12:14)

We have already established that the woman is Israel 'according to the flesh' from whom both Paul and Messiah were born 'according to the flesh' (Rom 9:3-5). We now therefore need to establish:

> (i) where were Israel to go as a people and as a nation after the vast majority had rejected Jesus as Messiah?
>
> (ii) what would happen to them there?

(iii) when was this unusual time period (1,260 days, three and a half years or 'a time and times and half a time') to begin and what is its significance?

'Into the Wilderness'

Firstly then, where? Notice the place God has 'prepared' for her during this time – she has lost the land and been forced to 'flee into the wilderness'. Remember, when they escaped Egypt, they came into the land after forty years in the wilderness of Sinai and Arabia.[31] However, this time it was not to be in a literal wilderness. Instead:

> 'I shall bring you into the wilderness of the peoples [or, Gentiles]…' (Ezek 20:35)

Just as Ezekiel had earlier prophesied of the Assyrian and Babylonian exiles, this Roman exile is not into the wilderness of Sinai but 'of the peoples' or Gentile nations. So where exactly did Israel go when they lost the land in 70 AD? Well, where did Jesus say they would go? 'Into all the nations' according to Luke:

> … they will fall by the edge of the sword, and will be led captive into all the nations; and Jerusalem will be trampled under foot by the Gentiles until the times of the Gentiles are fulfilled. (Luke 21:24)

This was the righteous judgment of God and, like Jeremiah (e.g. Jer 23:1-22), Jesus plainly warned all who would listen so that all who believed Him were able to escape with their lives (Luke 21:20-24. See also Matt 21:33-45 and

---

[31] *The Biblical Significance of Jabal al Lawz*, Charles A. Whittaker www.newprovidencebc.com/Mt%20Sinai/Biblical%20significance %20of%20Jabal%20al%20Lawz.pdf, 28 Mar, 2009

23:34-39). Those who didn't believe in that day faced the terrible consequences.

However, it also came about through the unrighteous anger of the dragon. Consider Satan's motivation now. Realising he has been thwarted and there is nothing he can do about the resurrected Messiah, he sees his inevitable doom but rather than give up, he turns all his hatred on the woman who bore Messiah. In the time of the sixth head, he inspired the Romans to destroy the nation of Israel, to sack Jerusalem and to disperse the Jewish people 'into all the nations.'

6. The Dragon's Hatred

Anti-Semitism

What was to happen to them 'in the wilderness'? It could have been that Israel, having achieved the birth of Messiah, simply faded away like so many other ancient peoples. However, God has promised that the nation of Israel will endure as long as the sun, moon and stars:

> Thus says the LORD, who gives the sun for light by day, and the fixed order of the moon and stars for light by night...
> 'If this fixed order departs from before Me,' declares the LORD, 'then the offspring of Israel also shall cease from being a nation before Me forever' (Isa 31:35-36).

Israel will *always* exist. Unfortunately, as long as Israel exists, Satan's hatred of the woman will also exist, manifesting in the earth as anti-Semitism – hatred of the Jews.

'He Persecuted the Woman...'

> And when the dragon saw that he was thrown down to the earth, he persecuted the woman who gave birth to the male child.
> And the two wings of a great eagle were given to the woman, in order that she might fly into the wilderness to her place... (Rev 12:13-14)

After the resurrection of Messiah, this hatred became even more extreme: 'the dragon persecuted the woman who gave birth to the male child' but with 'great wrath, knowing that he has only a short time' (Rev 12:12).

Of course, Satan's hatred is not directed only at Jews – as we saw earlier, the heavenly voice warns, 'Woe to the earth and the sea.' Satan hates all of God's creation but his hatred also has another particular focus as we saw in Genesis:

> I will put enmity between you and the woman, and between your seed and her seed; He shall bruise you on the head and you shall bruise Him on the heel (Gen 3:15)

The woman in Genesis was Eve but she foreshadows three distinct fulfillments of Satan's hatred. The first is a hatred of women in general, the second is seen here between the dragon and Israel and manifest on the earth as anti-Semitism, and the third is the enmity between 'your seed and her seed' – Satan's 'seed' are all those who follow him and hate 'her seed', the Child (John 8:39-47), and all who love Him (1 John 3:10-15).

One identifying feature of the dragon is therefore his particular hatreds: the hatred of women, the hatred of Israel and the hatred of Christians. His usually unwitting followers may indulge in any or all of these to varying degrees but this does particularly reveal the spirit behind fundamentalist Islam, given its attitude towards all three. It also reveals the spirit that tempted Martin Luther and will tempt every one of us at some time (1 Cor 10:13).

The Phenomenon of Anti-Semitism

However unpleasant we find this, we must learn and understand it, just as we must learn about AIDS, to avoid infection and to help anyone already infected.

There is no better example from which we can learn than Germany's experience. How, for example, did anti-Semitism subvert the vast defences available to the German people – their refined culture and history of rationality, philosophy, music, education, arts and technology – to deceive their nation into committing, in Winston Churchill's words, 'probably the greatest and most horrible crime ever committed in the whole history of the world', the Holocaust.

In 1986, the Norwegian committee awarded Elie Wiesel the Nobel Peace Prize, calling him a 'messenger to mankind' for his unrelenting efforts to ensure the lessons of the Holocaust are never forgotten. Weisel survived both Auschwitz and Buchenwald as a teenager, writing of his experience in a truly unforgettable first work, *Night*.[32] Prefacing the 2006 edition, Wiesel asks with forty-five years of hindsight:

> Why did I write it? Did I write it so as not to go mad or, on the contrary, to go mad in order to understand the nature of madness, the immense, terrifying madness that had erupted in history and in the conscience of mankind?

He concludes that he had to speak of what he saw: 'the witness has forced himself to testify. For the youth of tomorrow, for the children who will be born tomorrow. He does not want his past to become their future.' We therefore have to listen, unbelievable and horrific though we may find it:

> People could find no place in their consciousness for such… unimaginable horror… They did not have the imagination, together with the courage, to face it. It is possible to live in a twilight between knowing and not knowing.[33]

---

[32] Written in Yiddish and French, it was translated into English in 1958; new translation published by Hill and Wang, New York, 2006
[33] W.A. Visser 'T Hooft, quoted by Gitta Sereny, *Albert Speer: His Battle With Truth*, London: Macmillan, 1995, frontispiece.

This study attempts to step out of that 'twilight' into the light but we must each provide the courage to face it. In his profoundly challenging book *The Holocaust – Where Was God?* Jewish intellectual Arthur Katz calls on his people to grapple with…

> …the enigma of how we could be systematically annihilated, not by some primitive, backwater people, but by the most eminently civilised people on the face of the earth – Germany. It was a people with whom we had had a long-standing love affair, even to the point of celebrating Germany as *the* messianic alternative. Many Jews thought that, if all the world could be as German civilisation, then that would be the equivalent of Messiah's coming. We had lost the Biblical expectation long before and settled for something that was ethically, morally, and culturally impressive. To be brutally and bestially destroyed by that nation…, this is what twists the knife in right up to the hilt. The Holocaust was a shock against every thought of the twentieth century being an age of progress and human betterment or any other thing for which men hoped…
>
> Yet… few look to our Scripture to seek an explanation there [such as in Leviticus, Deuteronomy, Isaiah and Jeremiah]. Instead, we are raising up Holocaust museums because we hope that through education we will avert another such disaster. To our shame, we have not seriously taken into our consideration that the Holocaust of the Hitler period came at the hands of the most brilliantly educated nation. It shows just how misplaced our Jewish faith is – still fully convinced that the education of man will avert a repeat, while we ignore the explanation and ominous warnings of our own Scripture.[34]

---

[34] Introduction, p. iii, *The Holocaust - Where Was God?* Burning Bush Publications, 1998

   Dancing in the Dragon's Jaws

We therefore will look at the Scriptures and Germany. This is not to single out the German people for condemnation. After the war, Germany became one of the most repentant nations on earth as first, West Germany officially acknowledged their guilt, apologised and paid sixty billion dollars in reparations to Jews. Then in 1990, East Germany's first official act as a democratic nation was to pass the following resolution:

> We, the first freely elected parliamentarians of the GDR… on behalf of the citizens of this land, admit responsibility for the humiliation, expulsion and murder of Jewish men, women and children. We feel sorrow and shame, and acknowledge this burden of German history… Immeasurable suffering was inflicted on the peoples of the world during the era of National Socialism… We ask all Jews of the world to forgive us. We ask the people of Israel to forgive us for the hypocrisy and hostility of official East German policies toward Israel and for the persecution and humiliation of Jewish citizens after 1945 as well. [35]

What can we learn from how this remarkable nation was so thoroughly deceived by Hitler, or rather by the dragon inspiring him? History teaches and Revelation reveals that anti-Semitism will inevitably rise again, especially in the time of the seventh king with the ten horns. Today's newspapers are even now quoting al-Qaeda's chief spokesman, Sulaiman Abu Ghaith:

---

[35] Angelika Timm, *Jewish Claims Against East Germany (Moral Obligations and Pragmatic Policy)*, Budapest; Central European University Press, 1997, p. 79

My message to the Muslim youth is that al-Qaida
fighters are not the only ones meant to fight Jews ... it
is a duty on all Muslims to rise and defend their
religion.[36]

Why does he believe the Jews are attacking Islam? Other
headlines comment on the appearance of the 'New Anti-
Semitism' in Europe, particularly in France – 'new' because
it seems to the commentators to have no connection with
the 'old' reasons, emanating instead from young Muslim
immigrants identifying with the Palestinians and taking up
the battle for the land of Israel by bombing synagogues and
desecrating Jewish cemeteries in Europe.

The events of September 11, 2001, likewise brought hidden
attitudes to light in the U.S.A. Steven Accardi, a 42-year-old
clinical psychologist moved with his wife, Esther, and their two
young children to Israel:

> What pushed him to make the move was an incident
> in the street on the day of the attack in New York. He
> was parking outside his apartment in Monsey, New
> York, when a young man driving past yelled out of his
> window: 'Die!'
> Mr. Accardi spun his car around and caught up with
> the man. 'I screamed at this young punk, and then he
> hesitated and said: 'I want you people out of my
> country. You caused this.' I just stood there stunned,
> and as I went home, I thought about what he had said.
> Two hours after thousands of people had just been
> killed by an Arab terrorist, his first response had been,
> 'It's the Jews' fault.' In hindsight, I think this young

<hr>

[36] Associated Press, July 10, 2002

man, who uttered the anti-Semitic slur, was a shaliah, an emissary from God, saying, 'Get out'.[37]

Noa Hirsch, 22, a law student faced a similar reaction. She now lives in Jerusalem, studying Hebrew and law:

> 'On September 11, everything changed,' she said. 'I was going to a non-Jewish university, and I would get comments every day like: 'You Jews brought September 11 on us.' Never before in my life had I felt singled out as a Jew, and I had never felt so alone. So I thought to myself, where is the one place where I would feel welcome as a Jew? The answer: Israel. My family and friends are happy for me, even if they are worried.'[38]

To understand, let us start with how Germany was groomed for mass deception by their democratically elected National Socialist Party, the Nazis.

The Holocaust [39]

Consider the goal of the Holocaust – an openly proclaimed attempt at genocide, the annihilation of a whole race. There was no subtlety, no accidental 'collateral damage' of Jewish civilians, killed only because they had been unwittingly caught up in a battle-field. Instead the Nazis carefully sought out every Jewish child, every Jewish woman and every Jewish geriatric to die beside every unarmed Jewish man in the death camps. On 20 January, 1942, SS Reichsfuhrer Heydrich told his subordinates at the Wannsee

---

[37] Olim Aid International newsletter, 30/7/02

[38] Ibid.

[39] From the Greek *holos*, 'completely' and *kaustos*, 'burnt', the word was used in the Septuagint to translate 'burnt offering.' Also known as *Ha-Shoah* which is Hebrew for the Catastrophe, the Nazis called it *Die Endlösung der Judenfrage* – 'The Final Solution to the Jewish Question'

conference that their Final Solution was to 'comb Europe from east to west' to kill *eleven million* Jews.

Ten days later, his Fuehrer, Adolf Hitler, told the whole world that this war would not end 'as the Jews imagine, by the extermination of the European-Aryan peoples, but the outcome of this war will be the annihilation of Jewry.' Equally chilling was the way in which these aims were sometimes stated:

> He [Hitler] was capable of remarking quite calmly, between the soup and vegetable course, 'I want to annihilate the Jews in Europe. This war is the decisive confrontation between National Socialism and world Jewry. One or other will bite the dust, and it certainly won't be us.' [40]

Adolf Eichmann told his friend Rudolf Hoess, commandant of Auschwitz, that he felt obliged to destroy every Jew he could find, saying, 'Any compromise, even the slightest, will have to be paid for bitterly at a later date'. [41] Years later, hiding in Argentine, he explained to the Dutch Nazi journalist Willem Sassen, 'Personally, I never had a bad experience with a Jew… The enemy was not persecuted individually. It was a matter of a political solution, and for this I worked one hundred percent.' [42]

Was Eichmann just following Hitler's orders? 'I will jump into my grave laughing because the fact that I have the deaths of five million Jews on my conscience gives me extraordinary

---

[40] Albert Speer, *Spandau, The Secret Diaries*, London: Phoenix Press, 2000, p. 28
[41] John Bierman, *Righteous Gentile*, Bungay, Suffolk: Penguin Books, 1981, p. 16
[42] Bierman, p. 17

satisfaction'.[43] In this he presumably meant his corporate responsibility as a Nazi leader because he was personally responsible for transporting 'only' the following victims: [44]

Austria - 60,000
Belgium - 25,000
Bulgaria - 12,000
Czechoslovakia - 120,000
France - 65,000
Germany - 180,000
Greece - 60,000
Italy - 10,000
Poland - 10,000
Romania - 75,000
Scandinavia - 1,000
The Netherlands - 120,000
Yugoslavia - 10,000

How could this insane goal of total annihilation so nearly succeed? Hitler, Heydrich and Eichmann were never acting alone. As early as 1933, the Grand Mufti of Jerusalem, Haj Amin al-Husseini, aligned himself with the Nazis, moving to Berlin in 1941 and broadcasting to the Arab world that soon its 'hour of liberation' would arrive:

> Germany's objective would then be solely the destruction of the Jewish element residing in the Arab sphere under the protection of British power. In that hour the Mufti would be the most authoritative spokesman for the Arab world. It would then be his task to set off the Arab operations, which he had

---

[43] Bierman, p. 14
[44] Bierman, p. 15

secretly prepared.[45]

In Italy, Benito Mussolini complained to his mistress, Claretta Petacci, that Hitler was upstaging him in his anti-Semitism:

> I've been racist since 1921. I don't know how they can think that I'm imitating Hitler, he wasn't born yet… Those bloody Jews, they should be destroyed. I'll carry out a massacre like the Turks did. I'll build an island and put them all there…They don't even have any gratitude, recognition, not even a letter of thanks… They say we need them, their money, their help.[46]

She also recorded Mussolini's anger with Pope Pius XI who said that he was 'spiritually close to all Semites' and wanted Catholic marriages to Jews to be recognised.

Throughout eastern Europe, in Russia and the Ukraine, Poland, Lithuania, Latvia, Hungary, Romania and Yugoslavia, many openly nursed the same hatred for the Jews as Hitler and willingly served his purpose. This, incidentally, may explain why eastern Europe was left in the power of the Soviet empire at the end of World War II – Balaam, hired to curse the fledgling nation of Israel, refused to do so, instead predicting:

> Blessed is everyone who blesses you,
> And cursed is everyone who curses you (Num 24:9)

[45] Dr. Paul Otto Schmidt's minutes of Hitler's meeting with al-Husseini on Nov 28, 1941, Documents on German Foreign Policy 1918-1945, Series D, Vol XIII, London, 1964, p. 881
[46] Private conversations on 4 Aug and 11 Oct, 1938, recorded in the diaries of Claretta Petacci, published as *Secret Mussolini*, reported by the *Corriere della Sera*, Rome, 17 Nov, 2009.

Poland has only recently faced up to a massacre of 1600 men, women and children by their Polish neighbours on July 10, 1941.[47] A year after the Nazis were defeated, on 4th July, 1946, a Polish mob in Kielce killed forty two Jews including two young children when, having survived the Holocaust, they tried to return to their homes; four were teenagers en route to Palestine.[48]

In Hungary in early 1945, when Eichmann and the Nazis fled to avoid capture by the Russians, their work was eagerly taken up by the Hungarian Arrow Cross fascist movement who then murdered between ten and fifteen thousand Jews. One 'Death Brigade' was led by a Franciscan monk, Father Andras Kun, in cowl and cassock. He personally killed at least five hundred. At Father Kun's trial after the liberation of Hungary, a witness testified that he had lined up the staff and patients of a Jewish hospital and given the firing-squad the order, 'In the holy name of Jesus Christ, fire!'[49]

Nor were women exempt from this anti-Semitic insanity. Bierman records:

> Some of the most notorious Arrow Cross killers were women. A Mrs. Vilmos Salzer, described as a woman of good family and superior education, used to wear a grey riding-habit and brown boots as she went about her murderous business clutching a riding crop and a Thompson sub-machine gun. One of her milder forms of entertainment was to burn the sensitive parts of her female victim's bodies with a candle flame before killing them. She and Father Kun were among many Arrow

---

[47] Jan T. Gross, *Neighbours: The Destruction of the Jewish Community in Jedwabne, Poland*, Princeton University Press, 2000
[48] Gilbert, p. 251
[49] Bierman, p. 110

Cross Death Brigade leaders to be hanged after trial by
People's Courts.[50]

What kind of people could do such things? Auschwitz's
Rudolf Hoess wrote in his autobiography: 'I am completely
normal. Even while I was carrying out the task of
extermination I led a normal family life and so on.' Adolf
Eichmann was horrifyingly ordinary. At his trial in 1961,
one witness for the prosecution was Yehiel Dinur, a survivor
of Auschwitz. When Dinur saw Eichmann sitting in the
dock, he collapsed sobbing. Everyone assumed he was
overcome by his memories of Eichmann's evil but to the
astonishment of all he later explained: 'I was afraid about
myself. I saw that I am capable to do this... exactly like he.
Eichmann is in all of us.'[51]

Hannah Arendt wrote of the 'conspicuous helplessness the
judges experienced' while trying to understand Eichmann.
'The trouble with Eichmann was [not that he was a monster
but] precisely that so many were like him, and that the many
were neither perverted nor sadistic, that they were, and still
are terribly and terrifyingly normal.'[52] All she felt we could
learn was, in her extraordinary phrase, 'the lesson of the
fearsome, word-and-thought-defying banality of evil.'[53] She
could not detect 'any diabolical or demonic profundity' in
Eichmann or his colleagues, arguing against any 'satanic
greatness' in the Nazis and defining evil as possessing 'neither
depth or any demonic dimension' but 'overgrowing and

---

[50] Bierman, p. 110
[51] CBS *60-Minutes* interview by Mike Wallace, aired February 6, 1983
[52] *Eichmann And The Holocaust*, Penguin Books, 2005, p. 103
[53] Ibid. p. 90

laying waste the whole world because it spreads like a fungus on the surface.'[54]

Ms Arendt is obviously not alone in failing to understand the spiritual dimension but some saw more clearly.

The Starting Point

How did it all begin? Corrie Ten Boom, survivor of Ravensbruck, observed the change in her beloved homeland of The Netherlands:

> The true horror of occupation came over us only slowly. During the first year of German rule there were only minor attacks on Jews in Holland. A rock through a window of a Jewish-owned store. An ugly word scrawled on the wall of a synagogue. It was as though they were trying us, testing the temper of the country. How many Dutchmen would go along with them?
> And the answer, to our shame, was many. The National Socialist Bond, the quisling organisation of Holland, grew larger and bolder with each month of occupation. Some joined the NSB simply for the benefits: more food, more clothing coupons, the best jobs and housing. But others became NSBers out of conviction. *Nazism was a disease to which the Dutch too were susceptible, and those with an anti-Semitic bias fell sick with it first.*[55]

Even the strongest opponents of Nazism were not immune. On July 8, 1920, Winston Churchill had to speak to the British House of Commons after his colleague, Edwin

---

[54] Quoted by Idith Zertal, *Israel's Holocaust And The Politics of Nationhood*, Cambridge Middle East Studies 21, Cambridge University Press, 2005, p. 136
[55] *The Hiding Place*, New York: Bantam Books, 1984, p. 68, emphasis added

Montagu, the secretary of state for India who had spoken against a British Army massacre in Amritsar:

> Montagu's speech was a calamity. He was a Jew and there were anti-Semites in the house... He 'thoroughly roused most of the latent passions of the stodgy Tories', as one M.P. noted, and 'got excited... and became more racial and more Yiddish in screaming tone and gesture', with the consequence that 'a strong anti-Jewish sentiment was shown by shouts... Altogether it was a very astonishing exhibition of anti-Jewish feeling.' [56]

The Times reported that it was only Churchill's brilliant oratory that turned the House from this fierce animosity to accepting the obvious justice of Montagu's cause.[57]

> Churchill, an ardent Zionist since 1908, was unrepresentative of England's upper classes... The martyrdom of Jews in the 1940's would strip anti-Semitism of its respectability, but in the 1930's it was a quite ordinary thing to see restaurants, hotels, clubs, beaches, and residential neighbourhoods barred to people with what were delicately called 'dietary requirements'. As late as the 1950's the *Pocket Oxford Dictionary* defined Jew as '1. *n.* Person of Hebrew race; (fig.) unscrupulous usurer or bargainer. 2. *v.t.* (colloq.) to cheat or over-reach.' Contempt for them was not considered bad form. They were widely regarded as unlovable, alien, loud-mouthed, 'flashy' people who enriched themselves at the expense of Gentiles.[58]

---

[56] William Manchester, *The Last Lion - Visions of Glory (1874-1932)*, p. 693
[57] Ibid., p. 694
[58] William Manchester, *The Last Lion - Alone (1932-1940)*, p. 102

 Dancing in the Dragon's Jaws

Inspired by the Dragon

So what motivated all these anti-Semites, of whom Hitler was only the most prominent?

Rabbi Benjamin Blech writes that 'no one has yet been able to explain the profound depth of [Hitler's] hatred. Nor has anyone been able to adequately solve the mystery of how he was able to transmit this irrational hatred to so many of his people.'[59]

John's vision, however, not only explains the depth of Hitler's hatred and solves the mystery of how he could 'transmit' it to 'so many of his people' but also how the same hatred could be held by so many who were not 'his people' – they were all supernaturally inspired. Hitler himself described his world-view as the result of sudden personal revelations, telling Speer that when he was a young man in Vienna, 'the danger of Judaism had abruptly dawned on him.'[60] Hitler described his 'revelation' in some detail:

> Vienna appeared to me in a different light than before. Wherever I went, I began to see Jews, and the more I saw, the more sharply they became distinguished in my eyes from the rest of humanity... In a short time I was made more thoughtful than ever by my slowly rising insight into the type of activity carried on by the Jews in certain fields. Was there any form of filth or profligacy, particularly in cultural life, without at least one Jew involved in it? If you cut even cautiously into such an abscess, you found, like a maggot in a rotting body, often dazzled by sudden light – a little Jew. [61]

[59] *The Complete Idiot's Guide To Jewish History And Culture*, 2nd edition, Indianapolis: Alpha Books, 2004, p. 279
[60] Speer, *Inside The Third Reich*, 1970, p. 146
[61] Quoted by Michael Burleigh in *The Third Reich - A New History*, London: Pan Macmillan, 2000, p. 91

This then combined with two other 'revelations'. He believed devoutly in Darwinism (the subtitle of *Origin of the Species* was at that time *The Preservation of Favoured Races in the Struggle For Life*) and that Marxism/Bolshevism was just another Jewish conspiracy. The resulting paranoia caused him to see 'the Jew' as an assault on mankind's very existence. In 1924, he wrote in *Mein Kampf:*

> If, with the help of his Marxist creed, the Jew is victorious over the other peoples of the world, his crown will be the funeral wreath of humanity and this planet will, as it did thousands of years ago, move through the ether devoid of men. Eternal Nature inexorably avenges the infringement of her commands. Hence today I believe I am acting in accordance with the will of the Almighty Creator – by defending myself against the Jew, I am fighting for the work of the Lord.[62]

Speer struggled to explain it in natural terms:

> If you're asking me what it was in Hitler that could issue such an order for the murder of a people, then I can only tell you again, I don't know, and I'm quite convinced that no one else understands it either.[63]

However, Speer's secretary, Annemarie Kempf, had also watched Hitler closely:

> I, of course, have come to believe that human beings can be taken over by evil spirits. It isn't the sort of thing

[62] *Mein Kampf,* D.C Watt (ed.), University of London 1990, p. 60 Quoted by Burleigh, 2000, p. 92
[63] Gitta Sereny, *Albert Speer: His Battle With Truth*, London: Macmillan, 1995, p. 362

you could say to Speer. Although I think it is the only explanation for Hitler, in a way I too resist it. Because if, in one's inability to understand otherwise, one says Hitler, who after all started out by doing wonderful things for us, must have been taken over by the devil or whatever, then in a way one frees him of responsibility. One sets up a basis for compassion, and that has to be wrong. He has to have been responsible for what he did, just as we were responsible for what we failed to do, even if, closing our eyes to it, we did not 'consciously know' what it was.[64]

Of course, Biblically, being inspired by the devil does not free Hitler of any responsibility at all so Frau Kempf's conclusion is correct. External temptation appeals to what is already in our hearts (Jas 1:14-16) and we are all held responsible to cultivate love instead of hatred.

There has been a deep reluctance among modern historians to recognise this blatantly spiritual motivation. Michael Burleigh, Distinguished Research Professor in Modern History at Cardiff University, denounces this reluctance, asserting that the 'post-modern political religions' such as Bolshevism, Fascism and Nazism can only be truly identified by those…

> most dissatisfied with materialist explanations of political phenomena, or who treat ideas seriously, rather than as something secondary to 'facts' or to allegedly 'deeper' socio-economic structures, which on closer scrutiny explain rather little. As Bertrand Russell wrote, 'To understand Bolshevism it is not sufficient to

---

[64] Ibid., p. 363

know facts; it is necessary also to enter with sympathy or imagination into a new spirit.'[65]

This is why the Book of Revelation is essential reading for any wanting to understand our world today.

Notice where Hitler's revelation led him? Jesus spoke of 'an hour coming for everyone who kills you to think he is offering service to God' (John 16:2) and Hitler indeed saw himself as sent by Providence to be the saviour of the human race. He never lost his belief that Jews were the ultimate enemy, as can be seen in his final words, calmly dictated to his secretary, Gertrude Junge, just hours before his suicide:

> More than thirty years have passed since I made my modest contribution as a volunteer in the First World War, which was forced upon the Reich... In these three decades, love and loyalty to my people alone have guided me in all my thoughts, actions and life. They gave me power to make the most difficult decisions which have ever confronted mortal man... It is untrue that I or anybody else in Germany wanted war in 1939. *It was wanted and provoked exclusively by those international statesmen who either were of Jewish origin or worked for Jewish interests...* (emphasis added)

He then went on to make a chilling prediction:

> Centuries will go by, but from the ruins of our towns and monuments the hatred of those ultimately responsible will always grow anew. They are the people

[65] *The Third Reich - A New History,* London; Macmillan, 2001, p. 9

whom we have to thank for all this – international Jewry and its helpers. [66]

Bizarrely wrong in so many ways, Hitler was horrifyingly correct that hatred of the Jews 'will always grow anew'. Laurence Rees, an award-winning writer and BBC documentary producer, writes of interviews throughout eastern Europe after the Berlin Wall came down:

> In the Baltic states I heard people say how they had welcomed the Nazis as liberators [from Stalin]… I also encountered something more frightening as I traveled around these newly liberated countries, from Lithuania to the Ukraine and from Serbia to Belarus: virulent anti-Semitism. The old man in the Baltic states who had helped the Nazis shoot Jews in 1941 still thought he had done the right thing 60 years ago. And even some who had fought against the Nazis held wild anti-Semitic beliefs…
> What shocked me most was that these anti-Semitic views were not just confined to the older generation. I remember the woman at the Lithuanian Airways check-in desk … an army officer in his mid-20s … [67]

Behind every anti-Semitic attack in history, whether made by the ancient empires of Egypt, Assyria, Babylon, the Medo-Persians, the Greeks and the Romans, or by 20th Century political movements like Hitler's National Socialism of the 1930's and 40's and Gamal Nasser's pan-Arab attempts to exterminate Israel in the 1950's and 60's, whether made by European skin-heads or Islamic

---

[66] *Political Testament,* cited by William L. Shirer, *The Rise and Fall of the Third Reich,* New York: Simon & Shuster, 1960, p. 1124

[67] *Auschwitz: The Nazis and the Final Solution,* BBC Books, 2005, pp. 8-9

fundamentalists of the 1970's, 80's and 90's, or even the events of September 11th, 2001, behind all these attacks on the Jews or their allies has been a supernatural enemy, the great dragon, 'the serpent of old who is called the devil and Satan, who deceives the whole world.'

Anti-Semitism is undeniably demonic and one of the main political thrusts of Satan's work. Sadly, many bearing the name of the Lord, including whole denominations, have at times actively collaborated with Satan in these persecutions. Let us be very clear in our own minds: if any of us, even as professing Christians, allow ourselves to partake of any of the dragon's particular hatreds – the hatred of women, the hatred of Israel and the hatred of Christians – we are submitting to the spirit of the dragon.

Israel after Messiah

If we want to side with God, we must each therefore fully resolve a question that has beset the church from the beginning: what exactly was His attitude to Israel after they rejected His Son? As mentioned earlier, both the Orthodox and Roman Catholic Churches decided and taught for centuries that the Jews were the 'Christ-killers'.

With the sixteenth century Reformation rejecting much of Catholicism, we might have expected a change of attitude towards Israel but in fact, as we saw earlier, Martin Luther was also fiercely anti-Semitic, advocating in 1543 in his infamous pamphlet, *On The Jews And Their Lies*, such persecution as the burning of Jewish synagogues, schools and homes, forbidding the rabbis to preach, destroying prayer-books and confiscating property and money. Four centuries later, the Nazis quoted this pamphlet, even citing it in the Nuremberg trials as justifying the 'Final Solution'[68]

Luther and those who believed as he did actively prepared Germany for Hitler and there are many Jews today who still believe that Hitler was a Christian [69] because he was able to tap into church-promoted prejudice and hatred of them. As unpalatable as this may be to us today, we must not deny or ignore these horrible consequences of misunderstanding the Scriptures.

The Orthodox, Catholic and Protestant churches have all taught that God's attitude towards Israel, after their rejection of Jesus as Messiah, was utter rejection of them as a nation. A natural conclusion from this belief is that the church has entirely taken Israel's place and this idea has permeated the newer Charismatic and Pentecostal movements of today.

However, as we will see next, the Book of Revelation can correct us, telling us exactly *in typological form* of God's interest and purposes both for the people and the land:

> And the two wings of the great eagle were given to the woman, in order that she might fly into the wilderness to her place, where she was nourished for a time and times and half a time, from the presence of the serpent. (Rev 12:14)

We have yet to establish the timing and significance of the mysterious time period, 'a time, times and half a time', but having found where Israel was to go, 'into the wilderness of the peoples' (Ezek 20:35), we need to answer

---

[68] *Nuremberg Trial Proceedings*, Vol. 12, p. 318, Avalon Project, Yale Law School, Apr 19, 1946.

[69] See Appendix B: *Hitler And The Church*

'what was to happen to her there?' by seeking out the meaning of the eagle's wings.

'The Two Wings of the Great Eagle'

Some have seen here a symbol of American help for Israel because America's national emblem is the majestic, white-headed bald eagle. However, these wings had been used before to deliver Israel, over three and a half thousand years ago. Following Israel's exodus from Egypt and into the wilderness, God explained His role:

> 'You yourselves have seen what I did to the Egyptians, and how I bore you on eagles' wings, and brought you to Myself' (Ex 19:4)

In Deuteronomy, Moses explains further when he reminds Israel of what God had done for them:

> He [God] found him [Israel] in a desert land, and in the howling waste of a wilderness; He encircled him, He cared for him, He guarded him as the apple [or, pupil] of His eye.
> Like an eagle that stirs up its nest, that hovers over its young, He spread His wings and caught them; He carried them on His pinions (Deut 32:10-11)

When it is time for the eagle's young to fly, the eagle 'stirs up its nest'; it even dismantles the nest so that the eaglets have nowhere to go except out. Then, since the eyries are so high and the eaglets cannot yet fly, the young birds plummet, flapping frantically. The parent eagles, watching closely, dive down under the eaglets, catch them on their outspread wings and bear them up again, to try again and again until the eaglets learn how to fly.

What then did God do for the nation of Israel? 'He spread His wings and caught them, He carried them on His pinions.' As Israel were coming out of Egypt into the wilderness, they were being taught how to be spiritual people, how to fly. While they were learning and making their mistakes, God was catching them and bearing them up to try and try again.

Why the wilderness? Away from the pleasures of the world and distraction of other voices, God's voice can often be more readily heard. He has often used the wilderness in His dealings with Israel, in the time of Hosea likening the nation to an unfaithful wife whom He continued to woo:

> Therefore, behold, I will allure her, bring her into the wilderness, and speak kindly to her (Hos 2:14)

Returning, then, to Revelation 12:14, where 'the two wings of the great eagle were given to the woman, in order that she might fly into the wilderness to her place.' In the time of Jesus, Israel was again unfaithful, rejecting Him as her promised Bridegroom (John 3:29) so again God took her into the wilderness for a time in 'a place prepared by God' (Rev 12:6).

It is therefore beyond all doubt that at the end of the first century AD, God's grace and patience is still with the nation of Israel.

Summary of the Wilderness

We see that even after Israel as a nation rejected Jesus as Messiah, God did not reject them but there were serious consequences:

(i) The woman is sent away from the land into 'the wilderness'.

(ii) This wilderness is not that of Sinai and Arabia but 'a wilderness of the peoples' or 'all the nations' (i.e. the Diaspora, 'the scattered' among the Gentiles).

(iii) Satan continues to hate and persecute the woman so that, like Job, she loses everything but he cannot take her life

(iv) This particular hatred, inspired by the dragon, is today called anti-Semitism and is the root of the Holocaust.

(v) The seeds of the Holocaust were sown in part by otherwise godly Christians who misunderstood or ignored the New Testament revelation.

(vi) The purpose of the wilderness, besides its being a natural consequence, is that Israel may turn back to seek the spiritual realm of God.

7. 'A Time and Times and Half a Time'

1,260 Days

In this wilderness, far from normal sustenance, she needs to be 'nourished for a time and times and half a time.' We saw in considering Revelation 12:6 that this same period is also described as '1,260 days'. Since there are thirty days in a lunar month, this is forty-two months or three and a half years so we see 'a time' is one, 'times' is two, and adding 'half a time' gives us three and a half 'times' or years.

We also find '1,260 days' in Revelation 11:3 and 'forty-two months' in Revelation 11:2 and Revelation 13:5. Another parallel is found in the forty-two 'sojourns' Israel made during their forty years in the wilderness (Num 33) so, like the seven heads and ten horns, this particular length of time is a recurring theme – in fact, it is referred to in the Scriptures ten times and all refer to one and the same particular time in history. So what is it and why is it so mysteriously described?

This will take quite some explaining but it is worth every effort to understand because it is truly astonishing. Some readers may be familiar with some of the following but we will end up with a significantly different outcome or understanding from much of what is taught today, with several major inconsistencies at last resolved.

The answer begins in Daniel. The phrase 'a time, times and half a time' first occurs in one of his visions (Dan 7:1), dated approximately 550 BC, where an angel says of an unusual future king that:

he will wear down the saints of the Highest One… and
they will be given into his hand for a time, times and half
a time (Dan 7:25)

Daniel again hears the phrase a decade later (Dan 11:1)
when he hears an angel confirm that:

these wonders… would be for a time, times and half a
time… (Dan 12:6-7)

So Daniel is told this time period is that of a 'wonder' or
mystery but he is left wondering:

As for me, I heard but I could not understand; so I said,
'My lord, what will be the outcome of these events?' And
he said to me, 'Go your way Daniel, for these words are
concealed and sealed up until the end time' (Dan 12:8-9)

In other words, 'these words' would not be understood
until the time of their fulfillment. However, there is another
reference in Daniel to a period of three and a half years that
is easily overlooked: the second half of his famous '70th
week' and it is to this that John is referring in Revelation 12.

Daniel's 70th Week

In approximately 539 BC, Daniel was praying when an
angel named Gabriel appeared to him (Dan 9:1). Gabriel is
famous for appearing to Mary over five hundred years later
to promise the conception of Messiah (Luke 1:26ff) but we
should note he also announced His coming to Daniel.

Daniel's prayer had been that God would fulfill His
promise to bring the people of Israel out their captivity in
Babylon after seventy years (Dan 9:2-3). In response,

Gabriel reassures Daniel that God will do so but adds an extraordinary prediction which multiplies seventy years by seven:

Notice, the 'week' here is not a week of days but of years. Israel's calendar included not only seven-day weeks but also seven-year cycles (Lev 25:8-22) and Jeremiah's 'seventy years' was to allow the land to enjoy its Sabbath years (2 Chron 36:21).

This was a wonderful promise. Not only were Israel and Jersualem to be restored after the seventy years in Babylon but 'a decree to restore' would trigger a time period of seventy times seven (i.e. 490) years for 'your people (Israel) and your holy city (Jerusalem)' which would include the coming of their long-awaited Messiah. Specifically, He would come after 'seven weeks and sixty two weeks' (i.e. 7x7 plus 62x7 years) or 483 years after 'the issuing of a decree to restore and rebuild Jerusalem' so that the '70th week' is to be the week of Messiah.

There has been disagreement over exactly which 'decree' is meant because three Medo-Persian emperors made four different decrees:

However, to make a long story short, in about 458 BC, Artaxerxes made a decree [70] and 483 years later, in about [71] 26 AD (there being no year 'zero' between BC and AD) Jesus of Nazareth was baptised by John the Baptist leaving His work as a carpenter to begin His work as 'Messiah the Prince'. 'Messiah' (from the Hebrew, 'Christ' from the Greek) means 'the Anointed One' and at His baptism He

[70] The four decrees were made by Cyrus in 538 BC, Darius in 520 BC and Ataxerxes in 458 and 444 BC. These dates are necessarily approximate because of many variables including changing calendars. Today's Gregorian solar-based was only established in 1582 AD from the Julian solar-based (established 46 BC) while the Jewish luni-solar-based was used during the Second Temple (516 BC to 70 AD) and for three hundred years after that. This Jewish calendar, after two or three years of 30 day lunar months, added in a thirteenth month, plus another when spring was delayed, as decided by the Sanhedrin. See also Appendix C: *Dating Daniel's 70th Week* regarding Sir Robert Anderson's well-known but mistaken dating calculations.

[71] It is now accepted that Jesus was born between 6 and 4 BC since Herod died in 4 BC (Matt 2:1-15) after he had killed the boys of Bethlehem under the age of two (Matt 2:26). It is almost certain that the star which led the Magi to Israel and then 'stood over' Bethlehem (Matt 2:1-12) was an extraordinary movement of Jupiter in April, 6 BC (Michael Molnar, *The Star of Bethlehem: The Legacy of the Magi*, Rutgers University Press, 2000, www.eclipse.net/~molnar, 15 Dec 2008). Jesus was 'about thirty' (Luke 3:23) when He was baptised, hence 26 AD. This accords with John 2:20 supplying a date of 27 AD for His first year of ministry (i.e. 'forty six years' from the beginning of Herod's Temple renovations in 20 BC). Also, John the Baptist was baptising in the 'fifteenth year of the reign of Tiberius Caesar' (Luke 3:1) or 26 AD, since Tiberius became co-equal with Augustus in 12 AD (www.roman-britain.org/people/tiberius.htm, 11 Feb 2008) when Augustus sought to avoid a battle for succession before he died in 14 AD. Lastly, Eusebius writing in 325 AD was not always accurate but he did record from his perspective that the destruction of Jerusalem in 70 AD was 'full forty years' after the Lord's crucifixion which would then be 30 AD. (*Ecclesiastical History, Book 3*, Chapter VII, para 9)

was visibly anointed with the Holy Spirit while the Father announced it out loud from heaven (Matt 3:16-17, John 1:29-34).

This marked the end of the sixty-ninth week, fulfilling Dan 9:25, 'until Messiah the Prince'. However, after the seven weeks and sixty two weeks, i.e. in the 70th week, there was to be an astonishing turn of events:

> Then after the sixty two weeks the Messiah will be cut off and have nothing… (Dan 9:26)

Israel's long-awaited Messiah would be executed and lose everything. And not just Messiah:

> …and the people of the prince who is to come will destroy the city and the sanctuary. And its end will come with a flood; even to the end there will be war; desolations are determined. (Dan 9:26)

Jerusalem and the Temple would be destroyed again. This must have been utterly perplexing to Daniel but both of these extraordinary prophecies of Gabriel's were perfectly, dreadfully, fulfilled:

> (i) In 30 AD Messiah was 'cut off', crucified by the Romans outside Jerusalem.

> (ii) In 70 AD, 'the people of the prince who is to come' (i.e. the Romans) sacked Jerusalem and the Temple. 'The prince who is to come' was Titus, their general who became their next Emperor.

Notice, both of these events were to take place in Daniel's 70th week and this also needs some explaining.

'The Days of Vengeance'

Jesus plainly warned His hearers of the consequences of not recognising Him:

> When He approached Jerusalem, He saw the city and wept over it, saying, 'If you had known in this day, even you, the things which make for peace! But now they have been hidden from your eyes.
> 'For the days will come upon you when your enemies will throw up a barricade against you, and surround you and hem you in on every side, and they will level you to the ground and your children within you, and they will not leave in you one stone upon another, *because you did not recognise the time of your visitation*'
> (Luke 19:41-44, emphasis added)

He referred them to Daniel:

> But when you see Jerusalem surrounded by armies, then recognise her desolation is at hand… because these are *the days of vengeance*, in order that all things which are written are fulfilled (Luke 21:20-22, emphasis added)

And fulfilled they were, in terrible detail. An eye-witness, Flavius Josephus who was with Titus at the time, recorded:

> (403) So the Romans being now become masters of the wars, they both placed their ensigns upon the towers, and made joyful acclamations for the victory they had gained, as having found the end of this war much lighter than its beginning; for when they had gotten upon the last was, without any bloodshed, they could hardly believe what they found to be true; but seeing nobody to oppose them, they stood in doubt what such an unusual solitude could mean. (404) But when they went in numbers into the lanes of the city, with their swords drawn, they slew those whom they overtook, without mercy, and set fire to the houses

wither the Jews were fled, and burnt every soul in
them, and laid waste a great many of the rest; (405)
and when they were come to the houses to plunder
them, they found in them entire families of dead men,
and the upper rooms full of dead corpses, that is of
such as died by the famine; they then stood in a horror
at this sight, and went out without touching anything.
(406) But although they had this commiseration for
such as were destroyed in that manner, yet had they
not the same for those that were still alive, but they ran
every one through whom they met with, and
obstructed the very lanes with their dead bodies, and
made the whole city run down with blood, to such a
degree indeed that the fire of many of the houses was
quenched with these men's blood. (407) And truly so it
happened, that though the slayers left off at the
evening, yet did the fire greatly prevail in the night,
and as all was burning, came that eighth day of the
month Gorpieus [Elul] upon Jerusalem; (408) a city
that had been liable to so many miseries during the
siege, that, had it always enjoyed as much happiness
from its first foundation, it would certainly have been
the envy of the world…

(420) Now the number of those that were carried
captive during this whole war was collected to be
ninety-seven thousand, as was the number of those that
perished during the whole siege eleven hundred
thousand, (421) the greater part of whom were indeed
of the same nation [with the citizens of Jerusalem], but
not belonging to the city itself; for they were come up
from all the country to the feast of unleavened bread,
and were on a sudden shut up by an army, which, at
the very first, occasioned so great a straitness among
them that there came a pestilential destruction upon

them, and soon afterward such a famine, as destroyed them more suddenly.[72]

Photo 3 — Arch of Titus, Rome. Note the seven branched golden menorah looted from the Jewish Temple being marched into Rome with captive Jews.

As prophesied by Gabriel and confirmed by Jesus Himself, the seventy weeks 'decreed for your people and your holy city' included these terrible 'days of vengeance':

(i) Over a million dead from disease, famine and warfare.

(ii) The sacking of Jerusalem.

[72] From *The Works of Josephus, 'The Wars of the Jews'*, Book 6, translated by William Whiston, Hendrickson Publishers, 1987. Some such as Rabbi Benjamin Blech (p. 123) quote Tacitus' figures as 600,000 dead and 600,000 enslaved but Tacitus says only that 'I have heard that the total number of the besieged, of every age and both sexes, amounted to six hundred thousand' (*The Histories* 5:13) http://mcadams.posc.mu.edu/txt/ah/tacitus/TacitusHistory05.html, 28 Feb 2008

(iii) The desecration and destruction of the Temple.

(iv) The survivors exiled and dispersed world-wide, never to return.

(v) Jerusalem remaining under Gentile domination for the next two thousand years.

The 70th Week Covenant

Gabriel goes on:

> And He will make a firm covenant with the many for one week, but in the middle of the week He will put a stop to sacrifice and grain offering… (Dan 9:27a)

It is often taught today that this verse refers to the Antichrist making a seven year peace treaty with Israel, only to break it halfway through its term. This view is very widespread due to two extraordinary publishing phenomena. The first was Hal Lindsey's best-selling non-fiction book of the 1970's, *The Late Great Planet Earth,* which sold over thirty five million copies and was translated into more than fifty languages. The second is Tim LaHaye and Jerry Jenkins' *Left Behind* series, whose sixteen books published between 1995 and 2007 have sold over sixty five million copies and are being turned into feature films, a children's series and graphic novels.

Nineteenth century theologian James Bosanquet commented:

> Every fresh interpretation only adds to the force of our conviction that some radical error lies at the foundation of all our Christian interpretations and, till it is discovered, the 70 weeks of Daniel will remain unexplained and inexplicable to the comprehension of every unprejudiced inquirer. [73]

---

[73] *Messiah the Prince,* London, 1866

Here is one such 'radical error' – despite these one hundred million books to the contrary, Gabriel is not talking about the Antichrist but 'Messiah the Prince', the subject of the previous verse, who brought the 'firm (new, eternal) covenant' to 'the many', who are not just the people of Israel but the whole human race, as prophesied by Isaiah:

> 'My Servant will justify the many as He will bear their iniquities' (Isa 53:11)

And again:

> 'It is too small a thing that You should be My Servant to raise up the tribes of Jacob and to restore the preserved ones of Israel;
> I will also make You a light of the nations so that My salvation may reach to the end of the earth' (Isa 49:6)

Messiah's Week

The 70th week of years is therefore Messiah's and it is prefigured in five hugely significant events in Jewish thinking: Creation, Noah's flood, Israel's founding, Joseph's famine, and Solomon's building of the temple.

(i) Creation

Just as the original Creation took *seven days*, so too does the new Creation, beginning with the reconciliation of all who will accept Messiah:

> Therefore if anyone is in Christ, he is *a new creature*; the old things passed away; behold, new things have come. Now all these things are from God, who reconciled us to Himself through Christ and gave us the ministry of

> reconciliation, namely, that God was in Christ reconciling
> the world to Himself... (2 Cor 5:17-19 emphasis added)

(ii) Noah's flood

Noah and his family were given *seven days* to enter the ark before the rain started falling:

> 'Enter the ark... for after seven more days I will send rain
> on the earth forty days and forty nights; and I will blot
> out from the face of the land every living thing that I
> have made' (Gen 7:1 & 4)

In the same way, the whole world is given Messiah's week to be saved from destruction by believing and being baptised into Him (Mark 16:16). The apostle Peter wrote of this foreshadowing:

> ...when the patience of God kept waiting in the days of
> Noah, during the construction of the ark, in which a few,
> that is, eight persons, were brought safely through the
> water.
> Corresponding to that, baptism now saves you – not the
> removal of dirt from the flesh, but an appeal to God for a
> good conscience – through the resurrection of Jesus
> Christ... (1 Pet 3:20-21)

Notice, baptism corresponds to our entering the ark while God patiently waits for all who will to enter, before He judges the world. Peter explains further in his second letter:

> ...the world at that time was destroyed, being flooded
> with water. But by His word the present heavens and
> earth are being reserved for fire, kept for the day of
> judgment and destruction of ungodly men...
> The Lord is not slow about His promise, as some count
> slowness, but is patient toward you, not wishing for any
> to perish but for all to come to repentance (2 Pet 3:6-9)

(iii) the formation of the nation of Israel

Jacob worked *seven years* for both Leah and Rachel and celebrated the weddings for seven days (Gen 29:18-28) and then was given their two maid servants, Bilhah (Gen 30:3-4) and Zilpah (Gen 30:9-10). From these four women came the entire nation of Israel.

In the same way, Messiah is the Bridegroom (Matt 9:15, John 3:29) and He works for seven years for all who will become His bride:

> 'Let us rejoice and be glad and give the glory to Him, for the marriage of the Lamb has come and His bride has made herself ready' (Rev 19:7)

He also creates us into a new 'holy nation' (1 Pet 2:9) of both Jews and Gentiles who trust in Him.

(iv) Joseph's Famine

Joseph stored up excess grain for *seven years* to provide for the *seven years* of famine that afflicted Egypt and Canaan (Gen 41:28-49). Earlier betrayed by his own brothers and then Potiphar's wife, he had been raised from prison to the right hand of Pharaoh to save Egypt and his own family.

In the same way, Jesus was assigned Messiah's 'week' to save Jews and Gentiles. Also betrayed by His brethren and the Romans who crucified Him, He was raised from the dead to the right hand of God to accomplish this.

(v) Solomon's Temple

Solomon was *seven year*s building the Temple (1 Kings 6:38), using Jewish and Gentile workmen (1 Kings 5:13-16,

2 Chron 2:17-18). In the same way, Messiah is building a spiritual Temple:

> And coming to Him as to a living stone which has been rejected by men, but is choice and precious in the sight of God, you also, as living stones, are being built up as a spiritual house for a holy priesthood, to offer up spiritual sacrifices acceptable to God through Jesus Christ.
> (1 Pet 2:4-5)

Jesus likewise uses Jewish and Gentile workmen to build His house which consists of any who are willing to enter into His new, eternal covenant.

'But in the Middle of the Week…'

> And He will make a firm covenant with the many for one week, but in the middle of the week He will put a stop to sacrifice and grain offering… (Dan 9:27a)

Beginning His ministry in 26 AD, at the beginning of Daniel's 70th week, Jesus was crucified after three and a half years, 'in the middle of the week', which 'put a stop to sacrifice and grain offering' by fulfilling all the Old Testament sacrifices and making them no longer necessary:

> When He said, 'A new covenant', He has made the first obsolete. But whatever is becoming obsolete and growing old is ready to disappear (Heb 8:13)

The timing of Daniel's prophecy therefore looks like this:

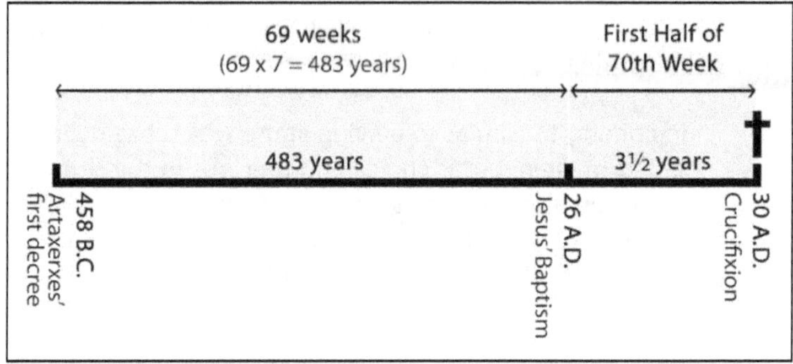

Figure 1 — Time line of 69 Weeks

Notice, the change in covenants was graphically demonstrated forty years later, in 70 AD, when the whole sacrificial system disappeared with the destruction of the Temple, the only place on earth where these sacrifices could be legitimately offered.

'Abomination of Desolation'

For the last two thousand years, the Jewish people and their greatest teachers have grieved the effect on their sacrificial system and tried to adjust. For example, Maimonides, a 12th Century rabbi and considered a second Moses by Orthodox Jews, taught that the sacrifices were now to be offered spiritually rather than literally until the Temple be rebuilt. However, they have not accepted *why* this happened, even though it was plainly predicted by the angel Gabriel to Daniel:

> '…and on the wing of abominations will come one who makes desolate, even until a complete destruction, one that is decreed, is poured out on the one who makes desolate' (Dan 9:27b)

An 'abomination' in the Scriptures is anything morally or spiritually repugnant, especially idolatry (Deut 7:25-26). In

   Dancing in the Dragon's Jaws

this instance, Gabriel says, there would be a particular abomination that would be the last straw, causing the 'complete destruction' of Jerusalem, 'the city and the sanctuary' as in v. 26, God's 'decreed' judgment 'poured out on the one who makes desolate'.

In other words, the nation of Israel would commit an abominable act that so pushed God beyond all endurance that He would withdraw His protection, allowing their enemies to defeat them and to desecrate the Temple: they would cut off Messiah the Prince, Jesus of Nazareth.

Jesus Himself also predicted it would happen:

> 'Truly I say to you, all these things shall come upon this generation.
> O Jerusalem, Jerusalem, who kills the prophets and stones those who are sent to her! ...Behold, your house is being left to you desolate!' (Matt 23:36-38)

This is also the point of the parables of the vineyard's tenants killing of the owner's heir (Matt 21:41) and of the wedding feast of the king's son:

> 'But the king was enraged, and he sent his armies and destroyed those murderers and set their city on fire'
> (Matt 22:7)

There are, as we will see soon, other occurrences of abominations of desolation both before and after the Crucifixion but, when you think about it, what could be more abominable to God than the rejection, persecution and execution of His only begotten Son?

'This Generation'

Why then was there a forty year delay between the abomination of the crucifixion and the consequent desolation of Jerusalem? Because forty years is the measurement of 'this generation' (Num 32:13, Psa 95:10) and God was giving them all the time possible to understand and repent. Forty also signifies a time of testing and judgment:

> 'You shall remember all the way which the LORD your God has led you in the wilderness these forty years, that He might humble you, testing you, to know what was in your heart, whether you would keep His commandments or not' (Deut 8:2)

'These forty years' were to 'humble' and 'test' Israel, to reveal their hearts.[74] So too were the forty years for Israel after Jesus, as Simeon prophesied:

> 'Behold, this Child is appointed for the fall and rise of many in Israel, and for a sign to be opposed… to the end that *thoughts from many hearts may be revealed*'
> (Luke 2:34-35, emphasis added)

Just as the forty years after the Exodus revealed what was in their hearts, so did the forty years after the Crucifixion. While most rejected Jesus and thereby fell, 'many in Israel' did 'rise' to faith in Him, as Acts records up to about 62 AD. (Acts 4:4, 21:20). They learned from His first disciples

---

[74] This testing and judgment is also seen in the forty-day flood of Noah and his family (Gen 7:12), the forty-day spying out of Canaan (Num 13:25), the forty penal strokes (Deut 25:3), Goliath's forty-day challenge of Israel's army (1 Sam 17:16), Jonah's forty-day warning for Nineveh (Jonah 3:4), the forty-day fasts of Moses (Ex 24:18 & 34:28), Elijah (1 Kings 9:8) and Jesus (Matt 4:2) and the forty-day appearances of Jesus to His disciples after His resurrection (Acts 1:3)

that with the fulfillment of Daniel 9:26, when Jesus was 'cut off and had nothing', that Daniel 9:27 meant Jerusalem's and their Temple's days were numbered. They were therefore well-prepared for the Roman siege of 68 AD:

> 'But when you see Jerusalem surrounded by armies, then recognise that her desolation is near. Then those who are in Judea must flee to the mountains, and those who are in the midst of the city must leave, and those who are in the country must not enter the city; because these are days of vengeance, so that all things which are written will be fulfilled' (Luke 21:20-22)

It may have seemed impossible for anyone to leave 'the midst of the city' after it was 'surrounded by armies' but in an astounding twist, the Roman general Vespasian temporarily lifted the siege when the emperor Nero died. He returned to Rome where he became emperor in December 69 AD, commissioning his son Titus to finish the job of crushing Jerusalem, so anyone believing Jesus' words was able to escape before the Romans renewed the siege and broke through in 70 AD.[75]

Notice too, Jesus' warning to 'this generation':

> 'The men of Nineveh will stand up with this generation at the judgment, and will condemn it because they repented at the preaching of Jonah; and behold, something greater than Jonah is here' (Matt 12:41)

---

[75] Recorded by eye-witness and Jewish historian, Josephus. He also blames the disastrous famine on murderous in-fighting amongst the defenders during which they set fire to their own grain stores which would otherwise have lasted for years (http://members.aol.com/FlJosephus2/warChronology6Factions.htm, 21 Feb 2008)

'The men of Nineveh' repented at Jonah's 'Yet forty days and Nineveh will be overthrown' (Jonah 3:4) but 'this generation' ignored the 'forty years' warning by Messiah Himself.

Multiple Fulfillments

Why is the crucifixion not widely recognised as an 'abomination of desolation'? Because there are at least *six instances* of abominations that have or will desolate Israel – two before Daniel and four after. (This will be properly considered in the next book in this series). Some prophecies can have several fulfillments when they identify a pattern or sequence rather than predicting a one-off event.[76]

The four 'abomination' prophecies of Daniel (8:13, 9:26-27, 11:31, and 12:11), written in mid-sixth century BC, refer to four then-future events:

---

[76] For example, notice how Matthew sees the fulfillment of Hosea 11:1:

> So Joseph got up and took the Child and His mother while it was still night, and left for Egypt. He remained there until the death of Herod. This was to fulfill what had been spoken by the Lord through the prophet: 'OUT OF EGYPT I CALLED MY SON' (Matt 2:14-15)

The full text of Hosea 11:1 being, 'When Israel was a youth I loved him, and out of Egypt I called My son', it may seem that Matthew is blatantly misquoting – the previous verses in Hosea clearly show God is speaking of the whole nation of Israel and their Exodus. How then can Matthew, by inspiration of the Holy Spirit, say this was a messianic prophecy fulfilled by Jesus? Because it is a type or foreshadowing – God calls *all* His sons 'out of Egypt' e.g. Abraham (Gen 13:1), Jacob (Gen 46:4), and Joseph (Gen 50:25) as well as the whole nation of Israel. Accordingly, Messiah had to be called out of Egypt too, as did the whole Early Church and us today (Rev 11:8). This is also referred to as 'thematic or prophetic recapitulation.'

(i) Antiochus Epiphanes' desecrating of the Temple in 168 BC, sacrificing a pig and erecting a statue of Zeus on the altar and thus fulfilling Daniel 8:9-27 and 11:31

(ii) the crucifixion in 30 AD which fulfilled Daniel 9:26

(iii) the desecration of the Temple in 70 AD which fufilled Daniel 9:27

(iv) one yet to happen (Dan 12:11). Paul, writing in about 50 AD, also predicts a particular man who will be confronted by the returning Lord Himself.

While Paul does not specifically refer to an 'abomination of desolation', his prophecy exactly parallels Daniel 11:36-37 in describing a future leader who sets himself up to be worshipped as God:

> 3. Let no one in any way deceive you, for [the day of the Lord] will not come unless the apostasy comes first, and the man of lawlessness is revealed, the son of destruction,
> 4. who opposes and exalts himself above every so-called god or object of worship, so that he takes his seat in the temple of God, displaying himself as being God…
> 8. Then that lawless one will be revealed whom the Lord will slay with the breath of His mouth and bring to an end by the appearance of His coming. (2 Thess 2:3-8)

First century believers were undoubtedly familiar with all of this, Paul asking them:

> Do you not remember that while I was still with you, I was telling you these things? (2 Thess 2:5)

Besides Paul's additional explanations, Jesus Himself on the day of His resurrection took the whole church on an extraordinary Bible study:

> Then beginning with Moses and with all the prophets, He explained to them the things concerning Himself in all the Scriptures (Luke 24:27)

> 'These are My words which I spoke to you while I was still with you, that all things which are written about Me in the Law of Moses and the Prophets and the Psalms must be fulfilled.' Then He opened their minds to understand the Scriptures (Luke 24:44-47)

Jesus went through 'all the Scriptures' and we know He included Daniel's prophecies because Matthew and Mark particularly draw our attention to them:

> 'Therefore when you see the abomination of desolation which was spoken of through Daniel the prophet, standing in the holy place (let the reader understand)…' (Matt 24:15)

> 'But when you see the abomination of desolation standing where it should not be (let the reader understand)…' (Mark 13:14)

This call to us, 'let the reader understand', means that every one of us needs to be on guard for a repetition of this abomination in our own lifetime. Some say this requires the rebuilding of the Temple, or the Third Temple, in Jerusalem which is being planned today by Jewish groups such as the Temple Institute. [77] Others argue that the Temple is the church (1 Pet 2:4-5) and that 'the man of lawlessness' will therefore make his claim within Christendom. Whichever view is right will be obvious closer to the time but we will revisit this issue when we come to study Revelation chapter 13 in the next book.

---

[77] http://www.templeinstitute.org

The Second Half of Daniel's 70th Week

So, for the first half of Daniel's 70th week, for three and a half years, Jesus of Nazareth was offering Himself only to the Jews as 'Messiah the Prince':

> 'I was sent only to the lost sheep of the house of Israel' (Matt 15:24)

> These twelve (apostles) Jesus sent out after instructing them: 'Do not go in the way of the Gentiles, and do not enter any city of the Samaritans; but rather go to the lost sheep of the house of Israel' (Matt 10:5-6)

This first half-week finished in 30 AD when Jesus was crucified. What then of the second half of Daniel's 70th week? Some have tried to find it in subsequent events, culminating in the stoning of Stephen (Acts 6:7-7:60) despite the text making no connection; others, not finding it there, have assumed it must be yet to occur but then also have to assume a gap of at least 2,000 years in the timing.

There is another, very different but more satisfying understanding. We, and the whole early church, were left with this apparent loose thread but 'a time, times and half a time' was already identified as 'a wonder' in Daniel 7:25 and 12:6-9. This is why it appears so prominently in John's revelation as he completes the rest of the picture for us all.

This mysterious time period also turns out to be the key to understanding one of the greatest mysteries of all time: the coming of Elijah. As we will see, this 'three and a half years', being a wonder, is not literal but typological or metaphorical, and describes the last two thousand years.

Note the term 'mystery' is not here describing a lost secret or an inexplicable matter, as in its most common usage, but in the Biblical sense, a profound truth requiring a particular understanding, often prefigured or foreshadowed. The *Zondervan Pictorial Encyclopedia of the Bible* explains the prophetic, predictive function of foreshadowing:

> These imply that the realities of heaven cast a shadow on the earth – a shadow which will in most cases later be replaced by actuality… that what God has ordained on earth is representative of what is in heaven but, for the present time, only a representation and not the reality itself…. (This) challenges the normal human pattern of thought, in which material objects throw insubstantial shadows: in this case, it is the spiritual, insubstantial but entirely real, which casts its shadow in a material form, in advance of its own final establishment. [78]

What is the connection between 'a time, times and half a time' and Elijah? Elijah just happened to call for a drought on the land of Israel for 'three years and six months' and Jesus Himself first taught about it in His own hometown. This was a profound revelation which we will consider next.

---

[78] Vol. 5, p. 368

Summary of 'A Time, Times and Half a Time'

We see then that John's 'a time, times and half a time' in Revelation 12:14 is a symbolic element in a recurring theme:

> (i) First mentioned in Daniel 7:25 (circa 550 BC) and again in Daniel 12:7 (circa 539 BC), it is identified as part of a 'wonder' or mystery.

> (ii) It symbolises three and a half years, being otherwise referred to as '1,260 days' (Rev 11:3 and 12:6) and 'forty-two months' (Rev 11:2 and 13:5).

> (iii) It is also the second half of Daniel's 70th Week.

Daniel's 70th Week prophecy is both astonishingly accurate and hugely significant:

> (iv) It predicts the coming of 'Messiah the Prince' would be 69 'weeks', or 483 years, after a decree to rebuild Jerusalem (Dan 9:24-25).

> (v) There were four relevant decrees by three Medo-Persian emperors but one decree, in 458 BC, brings us to 26 AD, when Jesus was baptised and publicly declared to be 'Messiah the Prince'.

> (vi) This week is foreshadowed in Creation, Noah's flood, formation of the nation of Israel, Joseph's famine, and Solomon's building of the Temple.

> (vii) It predicts 'Messiah will be cut off and have nothing' (v. 26) and that precisely in 'the middle of the week, He would put a stop to sacrifice and grain offering' (v. 27). Sure enough, after His baptism, Jesus ministered to Israel for three and a half years before being crucified in 30 AD and thereby made obsolete all further Temple sacrifices. This redundancy was put beyond all possible doubt by

the 'complete destruction, one that is decreed' (v. 27) of the Temple in 70 AD.

(viii) During this 70th Week, Messiah completes His side of 'a firm covenant', a new covenant, for 'the many', the whole human race. For the first half, however, He offered it only to the Jews.

(ix) His crucifixion was the final straw, 'the transgression' or 'abomination' that so grieved God that He allowed Israel's enemies to 'trample' their army and 'the holy place', thus leaving Israel and the Temple 'desolate' (Dan 8:13, 9:27).

(x) The desolation in 70 AD was also predicted by Jesus as resulting from Israel's not recognising 'the day of your visitation' (Luke 19:44) and not coming to the Son's wedding feast (Matt 22:7).

(xi) We are then left to resolve the 'wonder' of the second half of the week, a time period which just happens to recur in the mystery of Elijah.

8. The Mystery of Elijah

Jesus' Teaching

> 'But I say to you in truth, there were many widows in
> Israel in the days of Elijah, when the sky was shut up for
> *three years and six months*, when a great famine came
> over all the land' (Luke 4:25, emphasis added)

Thus began a teaching that hugely upset the people of His
home-town:

> And all in the synagogue were filled with rage as they
> heard these things; and they rose up and cast Him out of
> the city, and led Him to the brow of the hill on which
> their city had been built, in order to throw Him down the
> cliff (Luke 4:28-29)

What on earth could have so enraged the people of
Nazareth that they tried to kill Jesus for teaching it? Let us
put it in context. Jesus was attending His home synagogue
and had spoken from a passage in Isaiah which impressed
His listeners:

> And all were speaking well of Him, and wondering at the
> gracious words which were falling from His lips; and they
> were saying, 'Is this not Joseph's son?' (Luke 4:22)

They were pleasantly surprised by this 'local boy made
good' but then He said something that changed their
affectionate response into a murderous hatred – He pointed
out that throughout 'the three and a half years' of drought
and famine:

Sidon was Gentile territory and the woman to whom Elijah was sent was a Gentile! He then made it worse:

The Syrians were also Gentiles and, at times, fierce enemies of Israel, yet God had used Elijah's successor, Elisha, to heal this Gentile while by-passing all the Jewish lepers. Jesus was reminding them that God loves us all, regardless of nationality. Sadly, these Jews in Nazareth did not want to be reminded of their calling by God to be a holy or special nation in order to be priests to all the nations (Ex 19:5-6), to bless 'all the nations of the earth' (Gen 22:18). Instead they had become proud of simply being called. They were so enraged by Jesus' teaching that they 'cast Him out of the city, and led Him to the brow of the hill on which their city had been built, in order to throw Him down the cliff' (Luke 4:29) but He escaped them.

So what was Jesus saying? That God loves the people of Israel but also of every nation on the earth and *this was plainly seen in Elijah's 'three years and six months'*. Jesus also carefully, and for the very first time in the Scriptures, defines this as the exact length of time. Before this, the Scriptures only mentioned God speaking to Elijah 'in the third year' (1 Kings 18:1) but James the Lord's brother confirms it (Jas 5:17-18) so let us consider it more carefully.

Elijah's Drought

There had been other droughts in Israel as, for example, in David's time when there was a three year drought (2 Sam 21:1) or in Jeremiah's time (Jer 14:1). However, Elijah had a particular role during this time, very practically demonstrating the love of God to the Sidonian widow by ensuring that her bowl of flour and jar of oil never emptied (1 Kings 17:14) and even resurrecting her son (1 Kings 17:22). He also was responsible for starting the drought (1 Kings 17:1) and stopping it (1 Kings 18:42-45).

So what else is foreshadowed in this, Elijah's 'three years and six months'?

> (i) It signifies a period of judgment in Israel when God turns away from Israel's needs to instead help Gentiles.

> (ii) It signifies this period is not forever. When the time is over, He will work in Israel again.

> (iii) What God withholds from Israel and gives to the Gentiles is also significant. The rain is a symbol of the Holy Spirit (Hos 6:3) not falling on Israel, while God supplies Gentiles with the bread of His word, the oil of His Holy Spirit as well as supernatural healing and resurrection.

> (iv) Because we are considering a metaphorical foreshadowing rather than a literal future period of time, we should look for similarities in the later period rather than focusing on its duration. In other words, what happens to Israel in that time will be similar to what was happening to Israel during the three and a half years of Elijah's time.[79]

---

[79] Thanks to Tom Gillooly for this point.

This time period is also known as 'the times of the Gentiles'. Let us establish that now.

Jesus and 'The Times of the Gentiles'

In His final address, Jesus warns His Jewish disciples of the time soon to come when God would again leave Israel's needs in order to work amongst the Gentiles:

> 'When you see Jerusalem surrounded by armies, then recognise that her desolation is at hand... This people will be led captive into all the nations; and Jerusalem will be trampled underfoot by the Gentiles *until the times of the Gentiles are fulfilled*' (Luke 21:20-24, emphasis added)

Notice, Israel is to go into exile from their land 'into all the nations' (or, Gentiles; it is the same Greek word, *ethnos*). And when is this exile to end? When 'the times of the Gentiles are fulfilled' and Jerusalem is again in the hands of the Jews.

When did these 'times' start? When Jesus was crucified and resurrected; that is when He commanded His Jewish disciples to 'go therefore and make disciples of *all the nations*' (Matt 28:19).

Comparing Scripture with Scripture, let us put this text alongside Revelation 11:2. When John was writing at the end of the first century, Jerusalem had already been destroyed but in his vision, John is given a measuring rod and told to do some measuring:

> 'But exclude the outer court; do not measure it, because it has been given to the Gentiles. *They will tread under foot the holy city for forty two months*' (Rev 11:2, emphasis added)

So Jesus says Jerusalem will be trampled underfoot 'until the times of the Gentiles are fulfilled' and John says the Gentiles 'will tread under foot the holy city for forty two months.' We find then that 'the times of the Gentiles' and 'forty two months' are *the same period of time.* The symbolic 'time, times and half a time', '1,260 days', 'forty two months' and the last half of Daniel's 70th week are all likewise 'the times of the Gentiles'. So too is Elijah's drought of 'three years and six months' and it is also a 'wonder'.

Symbolic to Historical

We at last find here how to measure or translate this 'wonder' or symbolic time in historical time – we are simply to note *Jerusalem's status, whether it is ruled by Jews or Gentiles.*

'The times of the Gentiles' began when the Jews rejected Jesus as their Messiah in 30 AD This is also seen in Revelation 12:6, where the woman's time in the wilderness began after her Son was 'caught up to God and to His throne' (v. 5). The 'times of the Gentiles' were to end when the Jews regained Jerusalem – and that appears to have happened in 1967. Remember, although the people of Israel regained their land in 1948, this did not include the old city of Jerusalem. It was not until the Six Day War in 1967 that Israel regained Jerusalem for the first time since 70 AD. Those of us over forty, therefore, may have seen in our own life-times the ending of 'the times of the Gentiles'.

For the last almost 2,000 years, the Gentile nations have controlled or 'trodden under foot' Jerusalem so the 'times of the Gentiles' extend:

> (i) symbolically, from John's description, for forty two months

> (ii) historically, from Jesus' description, from 30 AD to at least 1967 – almost 2,000 years.

This time period is represented below in Figure 2.

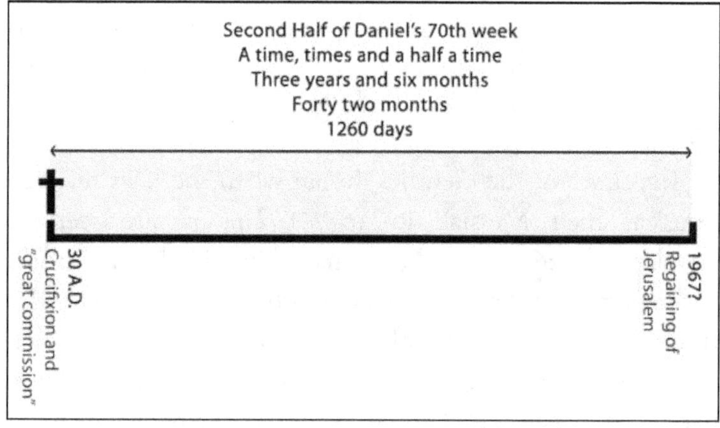

Figure 2 — The Times of the Gentiles

I acknowledge this is a radical new interpretation of both 'the times of the Gentiles' and 'a time, times and half a time'. Most of us have not been taught much about the times of the Gentiles, but the period is usually regarded as literal and historical rather than metaphorical. It is assumed to start from the Temple's destruction either by the Babylonians in 586 BC or the Romans in 70 AD. The 'time, times and half a time' is presented as a separate literal period in the future.

I often wondered how this could be since it means Jesus has to come three more times: firstly for the Rapture (the snatching away of the saints either before or in the middle of the Great Tribulation); secondly, to take His throne in Jerusalem to begin a thousand years reign; thirdly, to raise the dead and judge the world.

As each time requires Him to return, I worried about Hebrews 9:27-28 being explicit about TWO comings – He came the first time to die for our sins while His second coming will be the Day of Judgment (see also John 5:28-29, 2 Thess 1:6-10 and 1 John 3:2). All Christians agree on the first. It is usually the timing of the second coming that unnecessarily divides us.

I decided therefore to start with just two comings and to see if the other two could possibly be concurrent with the second rather than additional to it. To my amazement, I found that they can be concurrent if we allow for several texts being metaphorical rather than literal.

Here, then, is our exegetical (interpretive) choice: if we assume that *all* the second coming texts are literal, we end up with four comings, or three returns; if we accept several being metaphorical, we end up with just one return.

I suggest therefore that these phrases – 'the times of the Gentiles' and 'time, times and half a time' – are metaphors. Consider the correlation between the two (Luke 21:24 and Rev 11:2) and that everything else about the woman in the wilderness is undeniably metaphorical. The woman herself is a nation (Israel). The wilderness represents all the nations ('of the peoples'). The sun, moon and stars are Jacob's family in Joseph's dream; the wings of the great eagle depict

God's providence; and the flood sent to destroy her is Satan's attack.

As we will see next, they also fit perfectly into what Jesus taught about the two non-literal, indisputably metaphorical comings of Elijah:

> And if you are willing to accept it, John himself is Elijah who was to come... [and] Elijah is coming and will restore all things (Matt 11:14 & 17:11)

Jesus Himself said, *"If you are willing to accept it..."*

The Certainty of Uncertainty

There remains, fortunately, an element of uncertainty about these dates. Usually, prophetic dates are presented in broad brush-strokes, such as 'soon' and 'near'. When they are not (as in Daniel's 483 years 'until Messiah the Prince') the historical dates are not easy to establish.

We are supposed to be uncertain about end-time dates – God has built in uncertainty so that we must have faith at all times, and listen to the voice of the Holy Spirit in every situation. In other words, to stay alert (Matt 25:13).

While Jesus plainly expects us to 'discern the signs of the times' just as we read the sky to forecast the weather (Matt 16:3), He also warns us:

> But of that day and hour *no one knows*, not even the angels of heaven, nor the Son, *but the Father alone* (Matt 24:36, emphasis added)

Instead He calls us to recognise 'seasons', when particular conditions exist. For example, when the fig tree's branch has become tender and leafy, 'you know that summer is near' (Matt 24:32); when the gospel has been preached in the whole world, 'then the end shall come' (Matt 24:14).

Even in the timing of the regaining of Jerusalem, there is an element of doubt because of the Temple Mount. In 1967, when the Israeli troops finally recaptured their holy city, their general, Moshe Dayan, handed back the jurisdiction of the Temple Mount to the *Waqf*, the Muslim council, as a sign to the Arab League of Israel's peaceful intentions. This enraged Orthodox Jews because the Temple Mount, in the very heart of Jerusalem, is the only place on earth where those who want to keep the Law of Moses can ever rebuild the necessary temple.

It is therefore quite possible that until Israel has regained full control of the Temple Mount so that the Temple can be rebuilt, Jerusalem is still being 'trodden underfoot by the Gentiles'. However, consider the speed of Israel's restoration in the land: in the last 100 years, the Jewish population there has mushroomed from about 50,000 to 5.5 million; the Hebrew language has been resurrected from only synagogue and scholarly use into a national language; the nation itself has been recreated and most of Jerusalem has been regained. It does seem that for the first time in two millennia, the fig tree's branches are tender and leafy and about to bear fruit. It also seems that we have either just seen, *or are about to see*, the end of 'the times of the Gentiles'.

We can, however, be fairly certain that the time span of this vision did *not* begin in 1914 with the Jehovah's Witnesses, nor end in 70 AD as taught by others.

The Mystery of the Coming of Elijah

This mysterious time period set around an extraordinary city also includes a mysterious figure, the prophet Elijah. For thousands of years, the Jewish people have looked for Elijah to return as the forerunner of Messiah (Matt 17:10) as prophesied by Malachi (Mal 4:5-6). The annual Jewish Passover (or, *Pesach*) celebration includes a cup of wine which is poured but not drunk by anyone, being left for Elijah to drink when he comes. To this day, his return is one of the great mysteries of Israel.

Why Elijah? Why not the mysterious Enoch (Heb 11:5)? Or Melchizedek (Heb 5:11)? Among the many remarkable prophets in Israel's history, only Elijah compared to Moses as a miracle-worker – his prayers controlled the weather, raised the dead, called down fire from heaven and multiplied food. However, his ministry also had six typological features on which the mystery is based:

(i) Moses was the founder, Elijah was the restorer

Six hundred years after Moses founded the nation of Israel, it had divided into two kingdoms. The southern and smaller, then called Judah, was the faithful remnant, still holding fast to the covenant and the Davidic or Messianic dynasty; the northern kingdom, still called Israel, consisted of ten tribes and was ruled by Ahab and Jezebel who regularly entertained "450 prophets of Baal and 400 prophets of the Asherah" (1 Kings 18:19). Elijah was called to single-handedly confront them all on Mt Carmel, to restore the unfaithful nation of Israel to God.

(ii) Elijah raised the dead

The Law of Moses put to death, but Elijah was the first to raise the dead (1 Kings 17:22). Elisha later twice did the same but only because he had received a double portion of the spirit of Elijah, as is explained further in (iv) below.

(iii) the possibility of his return

Moses was buried by God Himself (Deut 34:5-6) but Elijah finished in spectacular style, being bodily taken up to heaven by a windstorm and a chariot of fire drawn by horses of fire (2 Kings 2:11). This left open the possibility of his return.

(iv) the double-portion of his spirit

Elijah's successor, Elisha, also had a spectacular ministry but only because he had received a double-portion of the spirit of Elijah:

> When they had crossed over, Elijah said to Elisha, 'Ask what I shall do for you before I am taken from you.' And Elisha said, 'Please, let a double portion of your spirit be upon me' (2 Kings 2:9)

When those following then saw Elisha part the Jordan river as Elijah just had, they recognised that 'the spirit of Elijah rests on Elisha' (2 Kings 2:15).

(v) 'the three and a half years' was started and ended by Elijah and its outcome was fruitfulness

Jas, the Lord's brother, highlights this outcome:

> Elijah was a man with a nature like ours, and he prayed earnestly that it might not rain; and it did not rain on the earth for three years and six months.
> And he prayed again, and the sky poured rain, and the earth produced its fruit (Jas 5:17-18)

Elijah was God's instrument to stop the rain 'on the earth' but then to restart the rain so that 'the earth produced its fruit'. Notice this refers particularly to the land of Israel.

(vi) Elijah is the forerunner of Messiah

According to Malachi, Elijah has to come before God can judge the world:

> Remember the law of Moses My servant, even the statutes and ordinances which I commanded him in Horeb for all Israel.
> Behold, I am going to send you Elijah the prophet before the coming of the great and terrible day of the LORD (Mal 4:4-5)

This prophecy, given about 410 BC, was God's final, authoritative prophecy as accepted by Israel. They were to be faithful to the Law and to keep looking for Elijah. This is why, in New Testament times, all of Israel were looking for the coming of Elijah as much as for the coming of Messiah, some thinking that Jesus was 'Elijah' (Mark 6:15).

But in what way was Elijah to come – literally or metaphorically? When John the Baptist came, they could see some physical similarity (2 Kings 1:8, Matt 3:4) so they asked him: 'Are you Elijah?' Of course, he was not literally so he replied 'No' (John 1:21). Jesus, however, says John was Elijah and that it takes particular insight to understand the first coming of Elijah, which is why many missed it:

> 'If you care to accept it, he himself [John] is Elijah who was to come. He who has ears to hear, let him hear' (Matt 11:14-15)

According to Jesus then, this coming of Elijah was metaphorical or 'a mystery', and John the Baptist fulfilled it.

Two Fulfillments

Jesus also predicts that Elijah is to come yet again. After the transfiguration, Peter, James and John have seen beyond all doubt that Jesus is the Messiah, but they do not understand how Elijah could have come before Him:

> 9. And as they were coming down the mountain, Jesus commanded them, saying, 'Tell the vision to no one until the Son of Man has risen from the dead.'
> 10. And the disciples asked him, saying, 'Why then do the scribes say that Elijah must come first?'
> 11. And He answered and said, 'Elijah is coming and will restore all things;
> 12. but I say to you, that Elijah already came, and they did not recognise him, but did to him whatever they wished. So also the Son of Man is going to suffer at their hands.'
> 13. Then the disciples understood that He had spoken to them about John the Baptist. (Matt 17:9-13)

In verse 12 Jesus says that John the Baptist did fulfill Malachi's prophecy but Israel failed to 'recognise him'. He also says in v. 11 that 'Elijah is coming and will restore all things' so there is to be a second fulfillment. The disciples must have found this hard to grasp because at the time they had no comprehension of Jesus' Second Coming either. It is much easier for us in hindsight, because we can see the logic in it: Elijah is to precede Messiah; Messiah has to come twice; therefore Elijah has to come twice.

This means everyone waiting for the Second Coming of Jesus should first be looking for the second coming of Elijah. It also means there have to be two fulfillments of Malachi's 'great and terrible day of the LORD':

How can that be? 'The great and terrible day of the Lord' is Judgment Day, the day when God will judge all the sins of all mankind of all time – surely that can only be in the future? No, because He has already done it *and* He will do it again:

> (i) The first 'great and terrible day of the Lord' was when Messiah died on the cross, accepting in His own body, soul and spirit all the wrath of God for all the sin of all mankind of all time (Jer 30:23-24, Heb 7:27)
>
> (ii) The second is the coming Day of Judgment, when Messiah comes again to judge all who have not had their sin dealt with by His death on the first Day (2 Thess 1:7-9, Heb 9:27-28).

What an extraordinary, eminently sobering thought.

So, before this second Day, Elijah has to come again. The question we now must ask is, if they did not recognise him in New Testament times, will we do any better? Their problem was that Elijah did not come in the way they expected. How are we expecting Elijah to come next time? If we are to recognise his second coming, we must understand the first so let us consider *in exactly what way* John the Baptist was Elijah.

The First Fulfillment: John the Baptist

John was *not* Elijah himself nor a reincarnation. In response to the question of the priests and Levites, 'Are you Elijah?' he said, 'I am not' (John 1:21). In what way then did Jesus mean that John was Elijah? In the exact same way as the angel who told Zachariah, John's father:

> And it is he [John] who will go as a forerunner before Him [Messiah] in the spirit and power of Elijah, TO TURN THE HEARTS OF THE FATHERS BACK TO THE CHILDREN (Luke 1:17)

Remember, following the translators' convention, the words are capitalised because the angel is quoting Malachi but he explains that John would come 'in the spirit and power of Elijah'. *Just as Elisha did* (2 Kings 2:9). And just like Elisha, there is a 'double-portion' but this time it is for two 'comings'. John, however, did no miracles so what was his 'power'? To 'turn the hearts' – this is why John came baptising for 'repentance' or turning.

And whom was he going to impact? At first glance, Malachi's prophecy about Elijah can seem to be limited to just fathers and children:

> And he will restore the hearts of the fathers to their children, and the hearts of the children to their fathers, lest I come and smite the land with a curse (Mal 4:6)

However, the angel adds the divine application and call to this prophecy:

> And it is he [John] who will go as a forerunner before Him [Messiah] in the spirit and power of Elijah, TO TURN THE HEARTS OF THE FATHERS BACK TO THE CHILDREN, and the disobedient to the attitude of the righteous; so as to make ready a people prepared for the Lord (Luke 1:17)

So the 'spirit of Elijah' was not limited to restoring loving relationships between fathers and children. That is only one example of the far greater and wider change that John was to effect. The angel tells us that he was actually to turn 'the disobedient to the attitude of the righteous' and to fulfill Isaiah's prophecy, 'to make ready a people prepared for the Lord' (cf. Isa 40:3).

One last point to note from Malachi's prophecy is the consequence to those who refused to be turned by Elijah/John the Baptist: God would 'smite the land [the land of Israel] with a curse'.

John's Effect

Ministering beside the Jordan River where Elijah had last been seen (2 Kings 2:7-11), John prepared Israel by 'preaching a baptism of repentance for the forgiveness of sins' (Luke 3:3), insisting on a change of heart and life-style. All who wanted to be baptised had to put right whatever was wrong in their lives, to care and share with the poor (Luke 3:11). Those in authority, such as soldiers and tax-gatherers, were to stop their abuses of power (Luke 3:12-14). The effects of this baptism were profound:

(i) Personal revelation from God

We see this in the crowds who were listening to Jesus when He talked about John:

> When all the people and the tax-gatherers heard this, they acknowledged God's justice, having been baptised with the baptism of John. But the Pharisees and the lawyers rejected God's purpose for themselves, not having been baptised by John (Luke 7:29-30)

Note these people and even the worst sinners, the tax-gatherers, were now able to see and 'acknowledge God's justice' in a way that the Pharisees and lawyers could not. They were now able to discern spiritual truth for themselves. As Paul says, genuine repentance 'leads to the knowledge of the truth' (2 Tim 2:25).

And, according to John the Baptist, as a direct result they became able to recognise Messiah:

> 'And I did not recognise Him, but in order that He might be manifested to Israel, I came baptising in water' (John 1:31)

On the other hand, 'the Pharisees and the lawyers' who refused John's preparation actually 'rejected God's purpose for themselves' and the resulting blindness caused them to miss not only the first coming of Malachi's Elijah, but also the first coming of Messiah. They then opposed Jesus' ministry and called for His crucifixion.

(ii) The beginning of the spiritual drought on Israel

Malachi warned that the rejection of Elijah's ministry would be a curse, which could include God withholding the rain (Deut 11:13-17). In this case, it was a spiritual drought: those who did not listen to John then failed to recognise Jesus as Messiah and thus did not receive the Holy Spirit after His resurrection (John 7:39).

Hosea predicted the Lord's coming in precisely these terms:

> 2. He will revive us after two days;
> He will raise us up on the third day
> That we may live before Him.
> 3. So let us know, let us press on to know the LORD.
> His going forth is as certain as the dawn;
> And He will come to us like the rain,
> Like the spring rain watering the earth (Hos 6:2-3)

This extraordinary messianic prophecy shows God's plan to restore us all to 'live before Him' through the resurrection 'on the third day' (v. 2) and the indwelling Holy Spirit coming to us 'like the rain' (v. 3). However, this restoration is only for those who are willing to trust in Jesus who was raised on that day (Rom 10:9).

Accordingly, Israel's rejection of Jesus as Messiah began the spiritual drought on them which was to last for 'the times of the Gentiles', the foreshadowing 'three and a half years' or, in our timescale, the last 2,000 years. This is why it was Elijah and not some other prophet or historical figure who was to prepare the way of the Lord.

To recap then, the results of Israel's rejecting the original Elijah were:

> (i) the beginning of a literal drought in Israel
>
> (ii) for literally three and a half years
>
> (iii) and God Himself turning away from their needs to help a Gentile widow.

The results of Israel's rejecting John the Baptist, coming 'in the spirit and power of Elijah', were:

> (i) the beginning of a spiritual drought in Israel i.e. the withholding of the Holy Spirit
>
> (ii) for a spiritual time of 'a time, times and half a time', three and a half years, forty-two months or 1,260 days
>
> (iii) and God turning away from Israel as a nation to help all Gentiles willing to trust in Messiah.

The Second Fulfillment

How then will Elijah come again? In writing this section, I am acutely aware of my own fallibility and the difficulties of this particular prophecy – only those having Jesus explain the metaphor could see the first fulfillment at the time. We can readily see that today because of hind-sight. To see the second fulfillment, however, puts us back into personal revelation and therefore careful judgment by each of us. Paul writes of this attitude being necessary in doubtful times. He had been asked about marriage and his response was:

> I have no command of the Lord, but I give an opinion as one who by the mercy of the Lord is trustworthy. I think then that this is good *in view of this present* [or impending] *distress*, that it is good for a man to remain as he is [i.e. if married, stay married; if single, stay single] (1 Cor 7:26, emphasis added)

The church was at that time facing terrible, literally murderous persecution, and single Christians did not leave behind widows and orphans. However, Paul's advice only applied at that time since the usual 'command of the Lord', as Paul taught elsewhere, was to marry and to have children (1 Tim 5:14). He also taught that the forbidding of marriage is demonic (1 Tim 4:1-3). He therefore concludes his advice to the Corinthians by urging them to 'let him do what he wishes, he does not sin', as long as each was following their own personal convictions of the Lord's will for them (1 Cor 7:36-37).

Accordingly, although the following seems plain to me, I submit it for your own personal judgment.

(i) Malachi's prophesied first coming of Elijah was spiritually discerned rather than seen by Israel's natural senses. John the Baptist came in 'the spirit and power of Elijah' and needed to be 'recognised', primarily by the effect of his ministry. Therefore Jesus' prophecy of Elijah's second coming will also need to be spiritually discerned by the effect of his ministry

(ii) Elijah's first coming in John the Baptist was 'to prepare the way of the Lord' by readying Israel to recognise Jesus as Messiah. Elijah's second coming will likewise be to prepare Israel for Jesus' second coming by helping them recognise Him before He returns

(iii) another effect of Elijah's first coming on all who would hear him was the restoration of not only loving relationships between fathers and their children but also righteous attitudes in general. Elijah's second coming will likewise have the same effect

(iv) Elijah's first coming in John the Baptist was to the nation of Israel – he made no attempt to reach the Gentiles. His ministry preceded Messiah and the spiritual drought in the people of Israel and the start of 'the times of the Gentiles' when the Holy Spirit began to rain on the Gentiles. It culminated in Israel losing their land and their city, Jerusalem. At the closing of this time, Elijah's second coming is also likely to be primarily to the nation of Israel, since they have been restored to the land and to Jerusalem, and it is his 'spirit and power' that brings the spiritual drought to an end.

This last point is only 'primarily' because of Jesus' exact words:

'All things' could also apply to 'all the nations' as well as to everything Israel needs restored. This would be consistent with 'all the trees' in another of the Lord's teachings:

> Behold the fig tree and all the trees; as soon as they put forth, you see it and know for yourselves that summer is now near. Even so you, too, when you see these things happening, recognise the kingdom of God is near. Truly I say to you, this generation will not pass away until all things take place (Luke 21:29-32)

We looked earlier at Jesus' parable about a fig tree being cut down because it had not borne fruit after more than three years (Luke 13:6-9). We saw then how He cursed a fig tree, symbolic of Israel, for being unfruitful (Matt 21:18-20) but here in His reference to the fig tree budding, He adds: 'and all the trees'. Indeed, the effects of Elijah's second coming may be the remarkable restorations taking place in many other nations in these days.

So will Elijah come visibly as a man like John coming in his 'spirit and power' in the restored land of Israel? Or will he be seen to have come invisibly and internationally by restorations in all the nations? We must be open to either or both until one interpretation becomes undeniable or the Lord Himself comes.

The Restoration of the Fig Tree

Just as the ministry of Elijah defines the 'times of the Gentiles', so too does the city of Jerusalem:

> Jerusalem will be trampled underfoot by the Gentiles until the times of the Gentiles be fulfilled (Luke 21:24)

There is no doubt that within the lifetime of many of us, Israel has 'put forth' leaves and blossoms but it has been gradual. In 1948, Israel was finally restored as a sovereign nation, using a restored Hebrew language. However, it was not until 1967 that Moshe Dayan regained Jerusalem in the Six Day War, only to hand back the Temple Mount to the Muslims. It may be that this prophecy is not actually fulfilled until that too is in Jewish hands.

Many argue, often from Deuteronomy 30:1-3, that Israel must repent before God will restore them to the land. They point out that the majority of Israelis today are not only still rejecting Jesus as Messiah, not only non-observant Jews, but openly secular humanists or atheists. This, they say, means today's restoration cannot be of God but must be of human striving. However, Israel's unbelief does not limit God's ultimate ability to act – He will do whatever He wants with the nation and land of Israel. *If any individual is there, they will be affected by whatever He does.*

Consider how He restored Israel from Babylon in fifth century BC First, Ezekiel was to speak to the land – not to the people but to the land:

> "Surely in the fire of My jealousy I have spoken against the rest of the nations, and against all Edom, who appropriated My land for themselves as a possession with wholehearted joy and with scorn of soul, to drive it out for a prey.

> Therefore prophesy concerning the land of Israel and say
> to the mountains and to the hills, to the ravines and to
> the valleys, 'Thus says the Lord GOD…'" (Ezek 36:5-6)

This prophecy was spoken to Edom, today's Hashemite Kingdom of Jordan which also tried to annex the West Bank while occupying it between 1948 and 1967. Ezekiel continues:

> 'But you, O mountains of Israel, you will put forth your
> branches and bear your fruit for My people Israel; for
> they will soon come.
> For, behold, I am for you, and I will turn to you, and you
> will be cultivated and sown.
> I will multiply men on you, all the house of Israel, all of it;
> and the cities will be inhabited and the waste places will
> be rebuilt' (Ezek 36:8-10)

He then explains exactly why God was restoring Israel to the land:

> 'Also I scattered them among the nations and they were
> dispersed throughout the lands. According to their ways
> and their deeds I judged them.
> When they came to the nations where they went, they
> profaned My holy name, because it was said of them,
> 'These are the people of the LORD; yet they have come
> out of His land.' (Ezek 36:19-20)

Notice, 'the people of the LORD' being 'out of His land' gives Him a bad name. The nations all ask how can God be the God of Israel when they have lost what He promised them?

> Thus says the Lord GOD, 'It is not for your sake, O house
> of Israel, that I am about to act, but for My holy name,
> which you have profaned among the nations where you
> went…

I will take you from among the nations, gather you from
all the lands, and bring you into your own land'
(Ezek 36:22-24)

Israel's faith was not the issue in that restoration. How about today's restoration? Since it was the rejection in the 1st Century of the first coming of Elijah and Messiah that brought the curse on the land and the consequent loss of Jerusalem in the first place, I believe the restoration of both must be the outcome of the second coming of Elijah to herald the second coming of Messiah.

The Restoration of the Land

Notice too Ezekiel prophesied to the land that it would...:

'bear your fruit for My people Israel... I will turn to you
and you will be cultivated and sown... and the waste
places will be rebuilt (Ezek 36:8-10).

Of course, this was initially regarding their return from Babylon but what if it is being recapitulated? Consider the condition of the land today, compared to 1867 when Mark Twain described it 'under the Ottoman crescent':

Here were evidences of cultivation – a rare sight in this
country – an acre or two of rich soil studded with last
season's dead corn-stalks of the thickness of your
thumb and very wide apart. But in such a land it was a
thrilling spectacle. Close to it was a stream... Miles of
desolate country whose soil is rich enough, but is given
over wholly to weeds....[80]

---

[80] http://www.mtwain.com/Innocents_Abroad/ 47.html and 48.html,
12 June, 2010

                    Dancing in the Dragon's Jaws

Of all the lands there are for dismal scenery, I think Palestine must be the prince. The hills are barren, they are dull of color, they are unpicturesque in shape. The valleys are unsightly deserts fringed with a feeble vegetation that has an expression about it of being sorrowful and despondent... It is a hopeless, dreary, heart-broken land...

Palestine sits in sackcloth and ashes. Over it broods the spell of a curse that has withered its fields and fettered its energies.[81]

Or to 1913, as portrayed in Sir Frederick Treves's illustrated 'account of a tour in Palestine':

On nearing Jaffa... what is there to see? Merely a low line of bare coast, treeless and blank... Of this it is possible to say little more than that it is not water.[82]

[Besides some orange groves and wheat fields en route to Jerusalem...] the vast Plain of Sharon, so far as the eye can reach, is practically treeless. Such hedges as exist are mostly of prickly cactus...[83]

The first impression of Jerusalem... So harsh, bleached, and colourless is the country round about that the city itself is a shadow of a rock in a weary land... the environs of Jerusalem are a dusty, ungenial limestone waste.[84]

Caesarea, the once proud seaport... is now a mere wraith, a formless drift of stones and dust tenanted by slum dwellers, and as Dean Stanley says, the most desolate site in the Holy Land.[85]

---

[81] Ibid., 57.html

[82] *The Land That is Desolate*, London; Smith, Elder & Co, 1913, p. 4

[83] Ibid., p. 20

[84] Ibid., p. 40

[85] Ibid., p. 156

> Nazareth... is a sorry country, for the land is bare,
> harsh and treeless. The slopes are grey with stones,
> while the misery of the place is deepened by the
> starving shrub which struggles to live among the rocks.
> Here is assuredly to be seen the poverty of the earth.[86]
> The country around the lake [Sea of Galilee] is
> characterless, monotonous and bare. It is a treeless
> country, grey with stone rather than green with grass...
> Only one town remains out of them all – the half-
> ruinous and wholly dirty town of Tiberias... The Plain
> of Gennesaret, still fertile and even luxuriant, but
> neglected and forsaken like the rest of the land that
> surrounds the sea.[87]

Today, the region's infamous malarial swamps are gone, there are over 200 million trees, one fifth of the land is nature reserves, the Biblical animals and birds are being reintroduced and Israel is famous for its exports of fruit, such as Jaffa oranges, vegetables and flowers.[88] Is this not what Isaiah describes?

> The wilderness and the desert will be glad,
> And the Arabah will rejoice and blossom;
> Like the crocus it will blossom profusely
> And rejoice with rejoicing and shout of joy.
> The glory of Lebanon will be given to it,
> The majesty of Carmel and Sharon (Isa 35:1-2)

Historical novelist James Michener makes an argument through one of his characters musing in 1964:

---

86 Ibid., p. 177

87 Ibid., p. 192-3

88 http://www.mfa.gov.il/MFA/MFAArchive/2000_2009/2001/9/Flora
%20and%20Fauna%20in%20Israel, 12 June, 2010

This was the staggering, incontrovertible fact: the other custodians [Arabs, Crusaders and Turks] had allowed the once sweet land to deteriorate, the wells to fall in and the forests to vanish; the Jews had brought the land back to productivity.[89]

Whether Ezekiel's prophecy is repeating or not, the restoration is undeniable. Perhaps those who deny any Biblical relevance to Israel today should note that the first century disciples were slow to believe in Jesus' resurrection until they saw with their own eyes:

> So the other disciple who had first come to the tomb then also entered, and he saw and believed. For as yet they did not understand the Scripture, that He must rise again from the dead (John 20:8-9)

So too we as 21st Century disciples may need to reconsider our understanding of the Scriptures because of Israel's 'resurrection'.

The Restoration of the Rains

As important as may be the restoration of Israel to their natural heritage, the land and Jerusalem, even more so is the restoration of Israel to their spiritual heritage. This is where the second coming of Elijah is essential, to end the spiritual drought in Israel:

> Elijah... prayed earnestly that it might not rain; and it did not rain on the earth for three years and six months. And he prayed again, and the sky poured rain, and the earth produced its fruit (Jas 5:17-18)

---

[89] *The Source*, London; Transworld Publishers, 1991, p. 868

We have seen that the ceasing of the rains is, in prophetic type, 'the sky' or Heaven withholding the Holy Spirit from Israel as a nation, though not from individuals who believe – every Jew who turns to Jesus as their Messiah will always receive 'times of refreshing from the presence of the Lord' (Acts 3:19). But now we see that the second coming of Elijah has the effect of his praying *again*: 'the sky' is to pour rain on the nation in the land of Israel and they will produce the fruit of repentance.

This exactly parallels Ezekiel's prophecy:

> 'Then I will sprinkle clean water on you, and you will be clean…
> *Then* you will remember your evil ways and your deeds that were not good, and you will loathe yourselves in your own sight for your iniquities and your abominations.
> I am not doing this for your sake', declares the Lord GOD, 'let it be known to you. Be ashamed and confounded for your ways, O house of Israel' (Ezek 36:25, 31-32)

God knew then they would repent after returning and He knows it will happen again today. Consider Zechariah's prophecy:

> And I will pour out on the house of David and on the inhabitants of Jerusalem the Spirit of grace and of supplication, so that they will look on Me whom they have pierced;
> and they will mourn for Him, as one mourns for an only son, and they will weep bitterly over Him, like the bitter weeping over a first-born (Zech 12:10)

This outpouring is of 'the Spirit of grace', which means it is necessarily undeserved, and 'of supplication', to help them pray. In other words, God will stir them to pray. As they genuinely seek His face, they will see God 'whom they have pierced', i.e. Jesus of Nazareth, the only Son and first-born of God: the Messiah. They will mourn and weep bitterly because they will at last understand.

As they then put their faith in Him, Zechariah goes on:

> In that day a fountain will be opened for the house of David and for the inhabitants of Jerusalem, for sin and for impurity (Zech 13:1)

There is already anecdotal evidence of God moving in Israel as many Jews are becoming 'completed' or Messianic Jews by accepting Jesus as Messiah. This may become the final fulfillment and in this way, the restoration of 'all things' to Israel will be completed. Or we may yet see in the land of Israel a man like John the Baptist, again preparing the way of the Lord, followed by an unprecedented outpouring of the Holy Spirit there.

What Could 'Elijah' Look Like Today?

Consider John the Baptist: an unlearned, untrained man who appeared without fanfare or great presentation skills. He dressed and lived simply (Luke 7:24-25, 33), and did no miracles. He did not initially proclaim Jesus as Messiah, even though he had come to prepare His way, recognising Him only after a personal revelation (John 1:29-34).

John's message was simplicity itself – *live as you already know you should*. He called on Israel to stop being religious and to start bearing good fruit. When asked what that meant exactly, he told them to share what they had, to be honest, to stop stealing, falsely accusing and grumbling. He also told them of God's love and forgiveness, the coming of Messiah and of Judgment Day, and he reproved King Herod for living immorally and wickedly (Luke 3:7-20).

We must not underestimate the effect of this. In urging the people of Israel to simply be 'honest and good' from the heart, John was actually preparing the way for the seed of Jesus' words to fall into 'the good soil' (Luke 8:15) which alone bears fruit.

So what of today? Elijah could appear in Israel and 'look' the same today. It is even possible that, like John the Baptist (John 1:31-34), he may not himself initially recognise or proclaim Jesus as Messiah.

Summary of Jesus' Teaching on Elijah

Malachi's prediction of the return of Elijah was the last recognised prophecy of the Old Testament and Jesus explained much that we need to understand:

> (i) He defined Elijah's drought as 'three years and six months' and pointed out that God ignored the needs of Israel to meet the needs of Gentiles (Luke 4:25-26).

> (ii) In 30 AD, He commissioned His Jewish disciples to 'make disciples of all the nations' (Matt 28:19), i.e. Gentiles, after predicting that Jerusalem would be 'trampled underfoot by the Gentiles' and the survivors dispersed into 'all the nations' (Luke 21:24), which happened in 70 AD. He also predicted the 'times of the Gentiles' would be fulfilled when the Jews regained Jerusalem (Luke 21:24), which happened in 1967, except for the Temple Mount.

> (iii) John adds that the Gentiles 'will tread underfoot' Jerusalem for 'forty-two months' (Rev 11:2) which is also 'three years and six months', '1,260 days' and 'a time, times and half a

time'. Daniel reveals this period to be part of a wonder or mystery; it also just happens to be 'half a week' of years and we are still looking for the second half of Daniel's 70th Week.

(iv) This means that 'the times of the Gentiles' are the same as the 'forty-two months'.

(v) Jesus then hands us the key to calculating 'the times of the Gentiles' from the status of Jerusalem – who has sovereignty, Jews or Gentiles? Typologically or prophetically, 'the times' are symbolised as 'a time, times and half a time' but historically 'the times' have been the last 2,000 years.

(vi) This typological 'three years and six months' were to begin and end with the two comings of 'Elijah'.

(vii) Elijah's first typological coming was fulfilled by John the Baptist but Elijah has to come again and 'restore all things' (Matt 17:11).

(viii) The original, literal Elijah's being taken up to heaven without dying leaves open the possibility of him returning but 'a double portion of his spirit' being passed on to Elisha foreshadows two comings of his spirit. This is why Gabriel said that John would prepare the way for Messiah 'in the spirit and power of Elijah' – John was not literally Elijah or a reincarnation of him but metaphorically and typologically 'Elijah'.

(ix) The two comings of 'Elijah' are also seen in Malachi's prediction that Elijah's coming would precede 'the great and terrible day of the LORD', the day when God will judge all the sins of all mankind of all time. Happily for us, there are actually two fulfillments of that day: the first 'great and terrible day' was the crucifixion of Jesus, when He died as the Lamb of God for all our sins; the second 'great and terrible day' will be when He returns as the Judge of all (Heb 9:27-28, 2 Tim 4:1).

(x) We should therefore be looking for the second coming of Elijah before the second coming of Jesus. If this is as mysterious as the first coming of Elijah, we may only recognise it in hindsight but I believe we are seeing it in the 'restoration of all things'.

(xi) Over the last one hundred years over five million Jews or Israelis have been restored to their own language of Hebrew, their own holy city Jerusalem, and in their own land which is no longer lying desolate but blossoming in the desert. Still needing to be restored are perhaps their Temple Mount, but certainly the rain of the Holy Spirit and the revelation of their Messiah so that the land produces its spiritual fruit, i.e. Jews trusting in Jesus.

9. The River and the Earth
Helping Israel

Returning now to Revelation 12, as mentioned earlier the eagle's wings, the time period, the river and the earth are all important symbols. We have established the meaning of the eagle's wings and the time period so we now come to the river and the earth:

> And the serpent poured water like a river out of his mouth after the woman, so that he might cause her to be swept away with the flood.
> And the earth helped the woman, and the earth opened its mouth and drank up the river which the dragon had poured out of his mouth (Rev 12:15-16)

The woman is kept in the wilderness but away 'from the presence of the serpent' which would have meant her death, or Israel's annihilation, so Satan sends a flood of water after her to destroy her there. 'The earth' however, comes to her aid and 'drinks up the river'.

For many Jews today, the thought of the earth helping them seems bizarre in the light of the last two thousand years. For example, Milton Steinberg in *The Making of the Modern Jew* [90] chronicles an unrelenting animosity from 70 AD to 1934:

> At no time during the period we have described did the world cease to exercise pressure on the Jewish world (through) political persecution, economic degradation and social exclusion…[91]

---

[90] Published by Bobs-Merrill Co, Indianapolis, 1934
[91] p. 122

After Israel was 'led captive into all the nations' in 70 AD and into Jeremiah's 'wilderness of the nations', it must surely have seemed the final blow in 135 AD when Roman emperor Hadrian sought to erase even their name from the map. After apparently provoking the Second Roman-Jewish War (132-135 AD) by banning circumcision and renaming Jerusalem *Aelia Capitolina,* he destroyed 985 villages, killed 580,000 Jews, banned the Torah, executed Judaic scholars, put an end to the Sanhedrin, forbade any Jew to ever enter the city, built a temple to Jupiter on the Temple Mount and finished off by renaming the land of Israel as *Provincia Syria Palestina,* i.e. a Syrian province named after the Philistines.[92]

Steinberg describes how the Jewish people were affected from the 4th Century by the Roman church coming to power in Europe, climaxing in the First Crusade[93] which began with the massacre in Rhineland of 10,000 Jews for refusing to be baptised and ended with Godfrey de Bouillon herding all the Jews of Jerusalem into a synagogue to be burned alive:

> Politically, as well as socially, the year 1096 marks a turning-point in Jewish–Gentile relationships. Not only did the Jew lose at last the friendship of the Christian, he lost also his own political status and his right of citizenship... By the thirteenth century the Jew was nowhere a citizen and everywhere a chattel. In each land he sojourned by tolerance and not by right... When Henry II of England wished to finance the Third

<hr>

92 http://www.absoluteastronomy.com/topics/Hadrian#encyclopedia, 18 Dec, 2008
93 It is estimated that one third of Europe's Jews were killed in the First Crusade (cf. Rev 12:4) www.aish.com/literacy/jewishhistory/ CrashCoursePart44.asp, 4 Mar, 2008

Crusade, he confiscated one-fourth of the movable property of his Jews. To ransom Richard the Lion-hearted, for whom Jews had little reason to feel affection, the small Jewish community of England contributed three times as much as the entire City of London. When the King of France found his treasury empty in 1306, he expelled all Jews, preempting their entire property, including debts owed to them by Christians.[94]

Often forbidden by law from owning land, and so discouraged from farming, and with the feudal system demanding Christian oaths to the overlords, the Jews were turned away from manufacturing which required membership of Christian guilds. The primary area left to them was international trading, hugely aided by their being scattered among the nations in the Diaspora. However, while shipping men and supplies during the Crusades, the Christians learned about trade routes and this time drove out the Jew into the despised professions of finance:

> In the tenth century, Jews were either farmers, artisans or merchants. By the fourteenth, they were universally notorious as usurers. No greater catastrophe ever befell the Jew than this shift in economic position. It confined him to the unwanted scraps of the world's economy or to those branches that were stigmatized by social disapproval. It exposed him to the hatred of the exploited masses. It opened him to the charge of parasitism...[95]

Forced to wear yellow patches or badges by the Fourth Lateran Council in 1215, Jews were increasingly confined to

---

94 Steinberg, pp. 66-68
95 Steinberg, p. 71

overcrowded, unsanitary ghettos and subject to curfews.[96] In Frankfurt, four thousand people lived in less than two hundred houses.[97]

Steinberg writes of only one oasis – Spain.

> Under a tolerant Mohammedan rule ... the period from the tenth to the fourteenth century has gone down in Jewish history as their Golden Age: Poets and philosophers, grammarians, scientists, Biblical commentators, lawyers and doctors – many of the finest talent and some of genius – followed one another in close succession… No other Jewry was as free or as wealthy and no other Jewry lived with such grace and refinement.[98]

The famous scholar and teacher, Moses Maimonides, was born here in 1131 and it is thought that up to 90% of the world's Jewish population were living in Spain.[99]

Incredibly, however, Mr Steinberg may have looked through rose-tinted glasses because the Jews were especially taxed as *Dhimmis* (non-Muslims) and even here, in 1066 in Granada, a Muslim mob crucified the Jewish vizier (chancellor) and massacred some 4,000 Jews.[100] Many therefore consider the Golden Age in Spain to have ended at this point, in the eleventh century.

The 13th Century saw the Muslims driven out and in 1250, Pope Innocent IV officially re-instituted anti-

---

[96] For example, the Ghetto of Venice was legally instituted in 1516 — see http://www.jewishvenice.org/ghetto/history.html, 3 Mar, 2008

[97] Steinberg, p. 77

[98] Steinberg, pp. 37-38

[99] http://www.geocities.com/Athens/Academy/8636/History.html, 4 Mar, 2008

[100] http://www.jewishvirtuallibrary.org/jsource/vjw/Granada.html, 12 May, 2008

Semitism, which in Spain culminated in 1391 with the massacre of fifty thousand Jews, and hundreds of thousands forcibly converted and baptised. In 1482, the infamous Inquisition was established, 'processing' 13,000 *Conversos* (secret Jews) during the first twelve years and putting many to death. Finally, in 1492, under the strong influence of the Grand Inquisitor, Tomás de Torquemada, Ferdinand and Isabella expelled every Jew from Spain.

The Reformation and Enlightenment brought the Jews no relief, not even from Voltaire or Goethe. Steinberg writes that it was not until the French Revolution of 1789 that the tide at last turned, but very slowly. It took until 1867 for the Jews of Austria to become the legal equals of Christians, with similar status gained in 1870 in Italy, 1873 in Switzerland and 1895 in Hungary.[101]

England had expelled all its Jews in 1290 and under Oliver Cromwell in 1656 began to welcome them back,[102] but only 'admitted a Jew to the House of Commons in 1858 and to degrees at Oxford and Cambridge in 1871.'[103]

It was no better in Eastern Europe. Almost half of the world's surviving Jews had moved to Poland, Ukraine, Romania, and Hungary driven by the Crusades and the Black Death (the bubonic plague of 1348-1349). Jews were scapegoated for the plague, and massacred in 'sixty large cities and one hundred and fifty towns and villages.'[104]

---

[101] Steinberg, p. 155

[102] http://www.jewishencyclopedia.com/view.jsp?artid=895&letter=C, 3 Mar, 2008

[103] Steinberg, p. 155

[104] Steinberg, p. 44. See also www.fordham.edu/halsall/jewish/1348-jewsblackdeath.html, 10 Mar, 2008

When the Cossacks, aided by Orthodox Christian Ukrainians, rose up against their Polish overlords in the Khmelnytsky Uprising (1648-1654), Sir Martin Gilbert records: 'Over 100,000 Jews were killed; many more were tortured or ill-treated, others fled...'[105] Forbidden to enter Russia until 1772, the Jewish community had created major centres of learning in Poland, only to be swallowed into Russia when Catherine the Great seized most of Poland in 1795. The Tsars were especially cruel, with Nicholas I in 1827 conscripting even Jewish children into the military. As mentioned earlier, in 1882 Alexander III propagated the May Laws which openly aimed to force one third of Russia's Jews to emigrate, one third to convert to the Russian Orthodox faith and one third to perish by starvation (note again the fulfillment of Revelation 12:4). The pogroms of 1881-1884 drove many to emigrate. Between 1880 and 1930, the Jewish population in the United States grew from 400,000 to four million.[106]

Open Confession

We who are Christians today need to learn and face the consequences of these vast injustices, all too often committed in the name of Jesus. From the earliest days of my becoming a follower of Jesus, I was horrified at being associated with the historical Church, especially the Crusades and the Inquisition. I pointed out to any who tarred me with the same brush that the perpetrators of these crimes against humanity had acted in open defiance of Jesus' teaching, as Milton Steinberg observed:

---

[105] p. 530, *Jewish History Atlas*, London, 1976
[106] Steinberg, p. 163

Nothing in history is quite so ironical as the contrast between the Mohammedan and Christian treatment of the Jew [in 10th Century, Spain]. By their very religion, Moslems are enjoined to intolerance... but Moslem practice was much better than its preaching. In the Christian world, on the other hand, conduct was far inferior to theory. The very heart and essence of Christian doctrine were ostensibly love and tolerance. In practice, no Christian love was wasted on Jews.[107]

Like it or not, all of us who bear the name of Christ stand indicted.

For many years, I reassured myself in our Western idealised individualism, where I am held responsible for nothing other than my own sins, even if I am benefiting from past injustices perpetrated by others e.g. by inheriting stolen property from previous generations. I was shaken from this view by the prayers of righteous individuals Nehemiah (Neh 1:4-11) and Daniel (Dan 9:4-19) where they acknowledged they were corporately responsible:

> 5. 'We have sinned, committed iniquity, acted wickedly and rebelled, even turning aside from Your commandments and ordinances.
> 6. 'Moreover, we have not listened to Your servants the prophets, who spoke in Your name to our kings, our princes, our fathers and all the people of the land...
> 9. 'To the Lord our God belong compassion and forgiveness, for we have rebelled against Him; nor have we obeyed the voice of the LORD our God, to walk in His teachings which He set before us through His servants the prophets.
> 10. 'Indeed all Israel has transgressed Your law and turned aside, not obeying Your voice; so the curse has

---

[107] Steinberg, p. 38

been poured out on us, along with the oath which is
written in the law of Moses the servant of God, for we
have sinned against Him' (Dan 9:5-10)

Accordingly, I now accept that we who are called Christians have clearly, in Daniel's words, 'sinned, committed iniquity, acted wickedly and rebelled', especially when we consider the history of Israel, and as a follower of Jesus, I ask for the forgiveness of the Jewish people.

Those of us who are Jews may need to consider and face what Daniel is quoting of Moses' astonishingly accurate prediction of what would happen to Israel in 'the wilderness of the nations':

> Moreover, the LORD will scatter you among all peoples,
> from one end of the earth to the other end of the earth;
> and there you shall serve other gods, wood and stone,
> which you or your fathers have not known.
> Among those nations you shall find no rest, and there
> will be no resting place for the sole of your foot; but
> there the LORD will give you a trembling heart, failing of
> eyes, and despair of soul. (Deut 28:64-65)

Moses has here perfectly described the last two thousand years.

'The Earth Helped the Woman'

> And the earth helped the woman, and the earth opened
> its mouth and drank up the river which the dragon had
> poured out of his mouth (Rev 12:16)

How then has 'the earth helped the woman' to avoid 'the river' from the dragon's mouth?

This prophecy has had several dramatic fulfillments, the first being 2,000 years ago when Titus destroyed Jerusalem. Daniel had prophesied that 'its end will come with a flood' after Messiah's death (Dan 9:26) and it did indeed. However, we see God's enduring love for Israel, scattered among 'all the nations' of the earth to be preserved as a people for two millennia. As Steinberg ruefully went on to acknowledge:

> At no time during the period we have described did the world cease to exercise pressure on the Jewish world. Political persecution, economic degradation and social exclusion *combined to drive the Jew to ever stronger internal cohesion...* It is interesting to speculate upon what might have happened had the Christian not been endlessly hostile but sympathetic. Would the Jew then have wrapped the cloak of his identity stubbornly around him, or would he, like the man in the fable, gradually have opened it, and when the sun became pleasingly warm, have discarded it entirely?[108]

He goes on to explain how this shaped the Jewish character in gregariousness, thrift, resourcefulness, philanthropy and intellectualism as the Jews devoted themselves to literacy and education.[109] This in turn directly contributed to their ability to rebuild the land of Israel.

Another dramatic fulfillment was just sixty years ago in World War II, when 'the earth opened its mouth and drank up the river which the dragon had poured out of his mouth.' Since one objective of this study is to understand

---

[108] Steinberg, pp. 122-3, emphasis added
[109] Ibid. p. 135

our times, especially the motivations, godly and demonic, we will now consider some examples.

In speaking of World War II, we can easily miss the true significance of the name – this was only the second time in all of human history that the whole world went to war. We can also think of the Holocaust as merely a by-product of Hitler's greed for land and empire but, as we have seen, one of his prime motivations was his belief in a 'Jewish-Marxist' conspiracy. Thus the serpent was, through Hitler, sending a river to sweep away the woman.

So consider this – although six million Jews died in the Holocaust, many more millions of Gentiles died in this satanic flood. Poland alone lost three million and the USSR over twenty million following Hitler's Operation Barbarossa in 1942. The greatest land invasion in history, it consisted of seventy five percent of the German field army, or over three million men, together with six hundred thousand of Hitler's allies.[110] His armies flooded into the Soviet Union only to be swallowed up by the vast steppes as 'the earth opened its mouth and drank up the river.'

This is not to say that the Soviets were knowingly or willingly helping Israel in the wilderness – far from it – merely that the whole earth was caught up in Satan's onslaught, and also fulfilled the prophecy of Isaiah:

> O Israel… I will give other men in your place and other peoples in exchange for your life (Isa 43:1-4)

Although to Americans, September 11, 2001, was unprecedented, it was actually just one more fulfillment of John's vision. Osama bin Laden's impassioned oratory

---

[110] Burleigh, 2000, p. 489

against the USA as 'the Great Satan' was not only to get American troops out of Saudi Arabia but also because of the USA's support for Israel. The 2,977 victims of 9/11 came from fifty-five different nations, as again 'the earth drank up the river' of the dragon's hatred.

Willing Helpers, 'Righteous Gentiles'

In all of the Nazi-dominated countries, however, many knowingly helped the Jewish people at great risk to their own lives. In The Netherlands, for example, Corrie Ten Boom and her family were caught and sent to Ravensbruck with only Corrie surviving. Her story is told in *The Hiding Place*,[111] and she is honoured as a 'Righteous Gentile' in the Avenue of the Righteous in Yad Vashem, the national Holocaust memorial in Jerusalem.

In Poland, Irena Sendler smuggled 2,500 Jewish children out of the Warsaw Ghetto before being captured by the Gestapo in 1943. Questioned and tortured, her legs and feet fractured, she was sentenced to death but rescued after her organisation, Zegota, bribed a guard and fabricated her execution. For fifty years her heroism was vilified as fascist by the Communist regime but Yad Vashem honoured her in 1983 and her story was finally told before her death in 2008.[112]

The remarkable Raoul Wallenberg, a Swedish diplomat in Hungary is likewise honoured, credited by Yad Vashem with saving some 15,000 Jews by issuing them specious protective passports. Tragically, Wallenberg was captured and imprisoned at the war's end by the Russians and,

---

[111] Random House, 1982

[112] http://www.irenasendler.org/facts.asp, 17 Apr, 2010.

according to famed Nazi-hunter Simon Wiesenthal, may still have been alive in 1979: 'We have so many Nobel Prize winners, you know, but I don't know of any other man whom I would rather nominate for the Peace Prize than Raoul Wallenberg.'[113]

In southern France the small Protestant village of Le Chambon-sur-Lignon became a haven for Jews fleeing from the Nazis and their French collaborators, saving between three and five thousand. In Denmark, King Christian X and his people saved 99% of their Jewish population, smuggling over seven thousand out of the country in fishing boats before the Nazis could deport them to the camps.

King Boris III and the Bulgarian people refused to obey Nazi directives and saved some fifty thousand Bulgarian Jews, which to Hannah Arendt was 'most surprising of all, in the belt of mixed populations where anti-Semitism was rampant among all ethnic groups and had become official governmental policy long before Hitler's arrival... I know of no attempt to explain the conduct of the Bulgarian people, which is unique in the belt of mixed populations.'[114]

Again in Hungary, when Budapest was liberated, tens of thousands of Jews emerged from their hiding places in Gentile homes, monasteries, convents and church cellars.[115]

What motivated these saviours? For some, it was simply the right thing to do but for most it was a direct outcome of their faith. Bulgarian bishop, Stefan of Sofia, declared publicly that "God had determined the Jewish fate, and men had no right to torture Jews and to persecute them." The

---

[113] John Bierman, *Righteous Gentile (The Story of Raoul Wallenberg, Missing Hero of the Holocaust)*, Penguin Books, 1982, p. 196
[114] *Eichmann in Jerusalem*, The Viking Press, 1970
[115] Bierman, p. 116

Dutch ten Booms acted because they were Christians, Corrie praying: "Lord Jesus, I offer myself for Your people. In any way. Any place. Any time."[116] Her father invited Jews to hide in their home with the words, 'In this household, God's people are always welcome.'[117]

As for the people of Le Chambon, recognising them as 'Righteous Among the Gentiles', the Holocaust Museum records:

> With their history of persecution as a religious minority in Catholic France, empathy for Jews as the people of the Old Testament, and the powerful leadership and example of their pastor and his wife, Andre and Magda Trocme, the people of Chambon acted on their conviction that it was their duty to help their 'neighbours' in need.
>
> The Chambonais rejected any labeling of their behavior as heroic. They said: "Things had to be done and we happened to be there to do them. It was the most natural thing in the world to help these people."
>
> After the round-up and deportation of Jews in Paris in July 1942, Pastor Trocme had delivered a sermon to his parishioners, 'The Christian Church should drop to its knees and beg pardon of God for its present incapacity and cowardice.'[118]

In Hungary, Lazslo Szamosi, himself Jewish and an extraordinary hero, recorded:

> Whatever any of the rest of us may have achieved, it was Wallenberg who was the driving force of the whole rescue operation. It was his idea to co-ordinate the

---

[116] ten Boom, p. 74
[117] ten Boom, p. 78
[118] www.yad-vashem.org.il/visiting/sites/chambon.html, 3 Mar, 2007

efforts of the Swedish, Swiss, Spanish, Portuguese missions, the Papal Nunciature, and the Red Cross. We all worked in close co-operation under his leadership.[119]

So what motivated Raoul Wallenberg? Miriam Herzog met him when he rescued her from one of the 'death marches', from Budapest to Austria. She had sneaked into a barn holding hundreds of women claiming Swedish protection:

> I didn't have a Swedish passport, but I thought it was worth a try and I had this tremendous will to survive, even though I was so weak from dysentery and wretched from the dirt and the lice that infested me, that all I could do was find a space on the floor and lie down. I don't know how much later it was – maybe days – but suddenly I heard a great commotion among the women. 'It's Wallenberg,' they said. I didn't know this name, but somebody told me he was a Swedish diplomat who had saved many Jews already. I didn't think he could really help me, and anyway I was now too weak to move, so I lay there on the floor as dozens of women clustered around him crying, "Save us, save us." I remember being struck by how handsome he looked – and how clean – in his leather coat and fur hat, just like a being from another world, and I thought, 'Why does he bother with such wretched creatures as we?'
> As the women clustered around him he said to them: 'Please, you must forgive me, but I cannot help all of you. I can only provide certificates for a hundred of you.' Then he said something which really surprised me. He said: *"I feel I have a mission to save the Jewish nation and so I must rescue the young ones first."*

---

[119] Bierman, p. 107

                    Dancing in the Dragon's Jaws

I had never heard of the idea of a Jewish nation before.
Jewish people, of course, but not a Jewish nation. Later
I was to think about this quite a lot.[120]

Wallenberg was motivated by a clear sense of mission, to
do what he could to rescue the woman in the wilderness
from the flood coming out of the dragon's mouth.

Even in very heart of Nazism, Berlin, the capital of
Hitler's Reich, journalist and historian Cornelius Ryan
recorded that in 1945:

> '...in tiny cubicles and closets, in damp cellars and airless
> attics... almost 3,000 Jews still survived. That they did
> was a testimonial to the courage of a large segment of the
> city's Christians, none of whom were ever to receive
> adequate recognition of the fact that they protected the
> despised scapegoats of the new order – the Jews.'[121]

In Germany, Oskar and Emilie Schindler rescued 1,098,
as told in Steven Spielberg's epic movie *Schindler's List*.[122]
The extraordinary Helmuth James von Moltke worked
undercover to counter the deportation and murder of Jews,
including alerting the Danes in 1943 and thereby saving the
lives of thousands. Betrayed and sentenced to death in 1945,
he wrote in his last letter to his wife, Freya:

> For what a mighty task your husband was chosen: all
> the trouble the Lord took with him, the infinite
> detours, the intricate zigzag curves, all suddenly find

---

[120] Bierman, p. 82, emphasis added
[121] Cornelius Ryan, *The Last Battle (Berlin 1945)*, Kent; New English
Library, 1984, p. 35.
[122] based on Thomas Kennealy's 1982 book *Schindler's Ark*

> their explanation in one hour… it has all at last
> become comprehensible in a single hour…
> Dear heart, my life is finished…This doesn't alter the
> fact that I would gladly go on living and that I would
> gladly accompany you a bit further on this earth. But
> then I would need a new task from God. The task for
> which God made me is done.[123]

This particular mission, the preservation of the Jews, came to its great fulfillment three years later. As a direct consequence and in recognition of the sufferings of the Jewish people in World War II, the international community by means of the United Nations finally upheld Israel's claim to their ancient land. On May 14th, 1948, Israel's first Prime minister, David Ben Gurion, was finally able to declare Israel a sovereign nation again.

'A River Out of His Mouth'

> And the serpent poured water like a river out of his
> mouth after the woman, so that he might cause her to
> be swept away with the flood.
> And the earth helped the woman, and the earth opened
> its mouth and drank up the river which the dragon had
> poured out of his mouth (Rev 12:15-16)

There is one more aspect of the river to consider from the Scriptures. Since water is essential to life, water often symbolises the Holy Spirit (John 7:38) or the cleansing words of God (Eph 5:26). However, as an overwhelming flood, it was a means of death (Psa 69:15, 1 Pet 3:20-21), and symbolised the righteous wrath or judgment of God (Hos 5:10). There is also a satanic equivalent to each of

---

[123] Quoted by Os Guiness, *The Call: Finding The Central Purpose of Your Life*, Thomas Nelson Inc., 1998, p. 239

these: demonic anointing, defiling words, untimely death and unholy wrath.

We all have a choice here. James points out that just as a spring produces sweet or bitter water, our mouths can bless or curse and he urges us to only bless (Jas 3:10-11). It was, therefore, no coincidence that Adolf Hitler's rise to power came on a torrent of words, combining promises of Aryan greatness with anti-Semitic bitterness. His Minister of Propaganda, Joseph Goebbels, had a doctorate in philology, the study of words. They used their extraordinary oratory and skillful propaganda to denounce and curse the Jews as the supposed source of Germany's economic miseries in the 1930's. Satan's anointing on their natural gifts made an almost irresistible flood, poured out on the earth to destroy the woman.

Are we today better prepared than the Germans of Hitler's day? We need to be. As Revelation 12 predicts, anti-Semitism will inevitably rise again and we will each need to recognise, as soon as possible and in our own societies, the symptoms of the disease described earlier by Corrie ten Boom:

> During the first year of German rule there were only minor attacks on Jews in Holland. A rock through a window of a Jewish-owned store. An ugly word scrawled on the wall of a synagogue. It was as though they were trying us, testing the temper of the country... Nazism was a disease to which the Dutch too were susceptible, and those with an anti-Semitic bias fell sick with it first.[124]

---

[124] ten Boom, p. 68

'The Rest of Her Offspring'

Having examined in some detail the mystery of the woman and the time she spends in the wilderness, we now come to the last verse of Revelation 12. We find that the dragon, having failed to destroy her and her Child, targets other victims precious to God:

> And the dragon was enraged with the woman, and went off to make war with the rest of her offspring, who keep the commandments of God and hold to the testimony of Jesus (Rev 12:17)

Not just any victims but 'the rest of her offspring', defined as 'those who keep the commandments of God and hold to the testimony of Jesus.'

Although the whole nation is personified as one woman, it of course consists of successive generations of innumerable individuals and before her Child was born, He was their primary purpose and destiny. However, from that time on, they all embarked on two diverging paths. The nation divided into those who 'hold to the testimony of Jesus' and those who do not.

Paul points out this was foreshadowed in Genesis:

> Abraham had two sons, one by the bondwoman and one by the free woman.
> But the son by the bondwoman was born according to the flesh, and the son by the free woman through the promise.
> This is allegorically speaking: for these women are two covenants, one proceeding from Mt Sinai bearing children into slavery; she is Hagar
> Now this Hagar is Mt Sinai in Arabia, and corresponding to the present Jerusalem, for she is in slavery with her children.
> But the Jerusalem above is free; she is our mother…

So every Jew who has rejected the new covenant mediated by Jesus is still under the old covenant, mediated by Moses on Mt Sinai. That is why the nation of Israel remained so long out of the land, because the curse of the Law still applied to them, and 'the present Jerusalem' (about 60 AD) was in slavery. On the other hand, every Jew or Gentile who was and is trusting in Jesus as Messiah and His covenant belongs to Mt Zion, 'the Jerusalem above' (see also Heb 12:22), and comes into the liberty of their inheritance as an heir of Abraham (Gal 3:28-29).

The earliest of 'the rest of her offspring' were therefore Jesus' first (Jewish) disciples and to them has been added everyone since, whether Jew or Gentile, who follows Him:

> While He was still speaking to the crowds, His mother and brothers were standing outside, seeking to speak to Him. Someone said to Him, 'Behold, Your mother and Your brothers are standing outside seeking to speak to You.' But Jesus answered, 'Who is My mother and who are My brothers?' And stretching out His hand toward His disciples, He said, 'Behold My mother and My brothers! For whoever does the will of My Father who is in heaven, he is My brother and sister and mother' (Matt 12:46-50)

'The rest of her offspring' are her first-born Son's brothers and sisters. That's the good news. The bad news is that that makes us the dragon's other primary target and we have been from the moment we first believed (1 Pet 5:8-11). Many of the Early Church's leaders were martyred, including Stephen (Acts 7:58-60), James, John's brother (Acts 12:2) and, after the Book of Acts was finished, Peter

(John 21:18-19) and Paul. In the next book in this series, looking at Chapter 13, we will consider this more closely.

'Hold to the Testimony'

In Revelation 12, another distinguishing feature of 'the rest of her offspring' is that besides 'keeping the commandments of God', they 'hold to the testimony of Jesus.' Of course, keeping God's commandments does not mean that they remain under the Old Covenant but that, being under the New, they listen to and obey His voice (2 Cor 3:2-6). Perhaps not so obvious is the wonderful truth contained in the description, 'and hold to the testimony of Jesus.' This is a phrase from the courts of justice and it calls us all to be judges, just as Jesus does:

> Why do you not even on your own initiative judge what is right? (Luke 12:57)

And Paul:

> I speak as to wise men; you judge what I say (1 Cor 10:15)

'Testimony' is an 'oral or written statement made under oath or affirmation' by a witness and, in every trial, judges have to hear the testimonies of witnesses, both for and against the accused. In judging what is true, they have to make a decision as to which witnesses are right and which are wrong; in other words, whose words are they to trust?

The rest of the woman's offspring are therefore seen to be not only living godly lives but holding to 'the testimony of Jesus.' That is, they are judging Him to be 'the faithful and true Witness' (Rev 3:14) who can testify in regard to all the issues of life. This is a wonderful truth. I have many times been plagued with doubts and not known what to believe. I love being allowed, indeed required, to make that choice of either accepting or rejecting what Jesus says. I have to choose to trust His words but am reassured, knowing that He has 'eyes of fire' (Rev 1:14) so that nothing can be hidden from Him, and that He is eternally reliable.

Summary of the River and the Earth

John's description of the earth helping the woman in the wilderness may seem bizarre, given that from 70 AD when she entered the 'wilderness of the nations' until today, there has been wide-spread and unrelenting animosity towards the Jews wherever they have gone. This has included:

> (i) Hadrian's attempt in 135 AD to expunge all trace of Judaism and even the name Israel from the map.
>
> (ii) The institutional churches' persecution from the 4th Century onwards.
>
> (iii) The Crusades of the 11th to 13th Centuries.
>
> (iv) The yellow badges of the 13th Century.
>
> (v) The Spanish massacres and scapegoating for the Black Death in the 14th Century.
>
> (vi) The Inquisition of the 15th Century.
>
> (vii) The European ghettoes from the 16th Century.
>
> (viii) The Cossack massacre of the 17th Century.
>
> (ix) The Polish and Russian pogroms of the 19th Century.
>
> (x) The Holocaust of the 20th Century.

Appallingly, most of this was done in the name of Jesus. This must be openly acknowledged and confessed as hateful, inhumane, disobedient and dishonouring of Him.

Milton Steinberg identifies some unexpected side-effects of these centuries of relentless oppression:

> this furnace of hostility ended up forging some remarkable Jewish characteristics of cohesion, gregariousness, thrift, resourcefulness, philanthropy and intellectualism.[125]

There have been some extraordinary fulfillments:

> (i) Daniel prophesied that Jerusalem's end in 70 AD would 'come with a flood' (Dan 9:26) and God has preserved the Jews among 'all the nations' for the last two thousand years.

> (ii) At the same time as the Holocaust, when six million Jews died (one third of all living on the earth at that time), 'the earth drank up the river' from the dragon's mouth by fighting and defeating Hitler at a cost to the Soviet Union alone of twenty million.

> (iii) More recently, the September 11 attacks on America as Israel's chief ally led to the deaths of bystanders from eighty different nations.

Thankfully, there have also been those who deliberately chose to help the woman in the wilderness:

> (i) During World War II, many 'righteous Gentiles' of 'all the nations' risked their and their families' lives, many or most motivated by their Christian faith, to hide and save many thousands of Jews.

---

[125] Steinberg, p. 135

(ii) In 1947, the only world body which represents 'all the nations', the United Nations, recognising the terrible cost to the Jews of not having their own land, voted to reestablish the nation of Israel.

Lastly, there are warnings for us today:

(i) The river can be a metaphor for words. In creating the Holocaust, Hitler and Goebbels used their propaganda skills to devastating effect, and this kind of river will not cease.

(ii) The last verse of Revelation 12, verse 17, describes the dragon's other targets as faithful Christians, those choosing to accept Jesus' words as true and reliable in every situation.

10. Israel's 'Partial Hardening' *Until...*

Jesus told His disciples that they were not to accept His testimony if He was the only witness (John 5:31). He commanded them to search out and listen to other witnesses (John 5:32-47), as did Paul, quoting Moses: 'every fact is to be confirmed by the testimony of two or three witnesses' (2 Cor 13:1).

This simple precept of Moses to the judges of Israel (Deut 17:6 & 19:15) is the most quoted Old Testament phrase in the New Testament.[126]

Accordingly, everything in the visions and symbols of Revelation are confirmed elsewhere in the Scriptures. What we have seen here in Revelation 12 in pictorial or metaphorical form about 'natural' Israel, the woman surviving in the wilderness or Elijah's drought, we also find in doctrinal form in Paul's letter to the Romans:

> For I do not want you, brethren, to be uninformed of this mystery, lest you be wise in your own estimation, that a partial hardening has happened to Israel until the fullness of the Gentiles has come in (Rom 11:25)

John's vision illustrates this mystery: the 'partial hardening' of Israel while 'the fullness of the Gentiles' is coming into the kingdom of God. Notice Paul warns all of us who are Gentiles (Rom 11:13) to not be wise in our own estimation (Rom 11:15), to stop us thinking that we are smarter than Israel because we have recognised Jesus as their Messiah and they have not yet. There is no reason for Gentiles to boast because

---

[126] Matt 18:16, John 8:17, 1 Tim 5:19, Heb 10:28

we have simply been receiving more 'rain', or help from the Holy Spirit, than Israel has been.

Paul explains this 'partial hardening' in some detail. In the two preceding chapters of 9 and 10, Paul has been talking about Israel's rejection of Jesus, and then he summarises:

> I say then, God has not rejected His people, has He? May it never be! ...God has not rejected His people, whom He foreknew...
> What then? That which Israel is seeking for, it has not obtained, but those who were chosen obtained it, and the rest were hardened (Rom 11:1-2 & 7)

What was Israel seeking? Righteousness or right-standing with God (Rom 9:30-31 & 10:3). Who are 'those who were chosen', who 'obtained it'? Those who accepted His Son as the sacrifice for their sins, the offer being made first to the Jews and then to the Gentiles (Rom 1:16).

But what does Paul say of 'His people' who rejected His Son?

> The rest were hardened; just as it is written, 'God gave them a spirit of stupor, eyes to see not and ears to hear not, down to this very day' (Rom 11:7-8)

Does this mean that God has rejected them and made it impossible for them to repent? Not at all. The hardening is only 'partial' and if any Jew wants to turn to Jesus, they still can. Many have, even rabbis. Despite long years of being warned against turning to Him, many have read the Old Testament Messianic prophecies, especially Isaiah 53 and Daniel 9, and recognised Jesus of Nazareth as the only possible fulfillment. Israel's main problems have been either a misguided group loyalty ('We are Jews and we do not accept Jesus') or the belief that those who call themselves

Christians – like the Crusaders, the Grand Inquisitors, or Adolf Hitler – accurately represent Him.

Some may think this 'partial hardening' means that some Jews, a part of the nation, have been completely hardened so they cannot turn to Jesus and that some Jews have not been hardened, so they can. God does not work like that. 'Partial' is meant in the same way that Paul says of us all:

> We know in part, and we prophesy in part (1 Cor 13:9)

All of 'Israel according to the flesh' who had rejected Jesus as Messiah became only 'partially' hardened by their choice. In Rom 11:8, Paul describes the 'partial hardening' as fulfilling Old Testament prophecies of 'a spirit of stupor' or 'deep sleep' (Isa 29:10) and 'eyes to see not and ears to hear not' (Deut 29:4). However, individual Jews have always been able to rouse themselves (Eph 5:14). 'Eyes to see not', or spiritual blindness, is a consequence of individuals refusing to be born again as Jesus tells us:

> Truly, truly, I say to you, unless one is born again, he cannot see the kingdom of God (John 3:3)

Spiritual deafness also is a consequence of 'selective hearing', of hearing 'with the crowd.' Choosing to hear only what you want to hear, or what your group wants to hear, means you choose to remain partially deaf. Any who choose to stand with God, despite anybody or everybody else, will hear Him. As Jesus tells us:

> He who is of God hears the words of God (John 8:47)

However, despite this ability of individual Israelis to accept Jesus as Messiah, the Holy Spirit predicted what we have seen over the last two thousand years – that as a nation, Israel has not accepted Jesus as Messiah. But all that is about to change.

The End of This Mystery

We read earlier that Paul saw a clear end to this state of affairs:

> ... a partial hardening has happened to Israel *until* the fullness of the Gentiles has come in (Rom 11:25, emphasis added)

This 'until' necessarily means the 'partial hardening' will stop occurring in Israel. Moreover, since 'the times of the Gentiles' are coming to a close in our days, we should even now be watching for this change in Israel. Paul was emphatic about this future dramatic about-turn in Israel:

> Again I ask: did they [Israel] stumble so as to fall beyond recovery? Not at all! Because of their transgression, salvation has come to the Gentiles, to make Israel envious. But if their transgression means riches for the world, and their loss means riches for the Gentiles, how much greater riches will their fulfillment [*lit.* fullness] bring! (Rom 11:11-12 *NIV*)

Notice the two 'fullnesses' and their timing – after the 'fullness of the Gentiles has come in' to the kingdom of God, there is also to be a 'fullness' of Israel. 'Fullness' in English, Hebrew (*melo*) and Greek (*pleroma*) has a sense of richness, satisfaction, fulfillment, completion, and is used in the Scriptures of people, places, time and numbers. We see here, therefore, a remarkable coinciding of all of these meanings – the fullness of the Gentiles and the fullness of

Israel are to be in quantity and in quality which, in turn, reveal that it will be 'the fullness of time.'

This time could not have been in the first century AD because Jesus prophesied:

> And this gospel of the kingdom shall be preached in the whole world for a witness to *all the nations*, and *then* the end shall come (Matt 24:14, emphasis added)

The 'fullness of the Gentiles' therefore refers to people of 'all the nations' believing 'this gospel of the kingdom' and that simply could not happen until it had been 'preached in the whole world'. This has been found to be even more difficult than we might think as 'the whole world' uses 6,912 living languages. Papua New Guinea alone has had 830 languages, 820 of which are still in use while 10 have become extinct.[127] However, for the first time in all of recorded history, it is becoming possible to preach in every one of them.[128] Of course, this fullness is not just of numbers or quantity but also of quality, consisting of genuine believers of 'every tribe and tongue and people and nation' (Rev 5:9).

It also refers to the fullness of the quality of the church of God, vastly improved by our return to 'the gospel of the kingdom.' This includes our relationship to the King, the authority of the Scriptures, justification by faith, believers' baptism, the priesthood of all believers, the gifts of the

---

[127] www.ethnologue.com/home.asp and ww.ethnologue.com/show_country.asp?name=PG, 7 Apr, 2009

[128] Besides preaching, in 2006 the United Bible Societies reported that the complete Bible is now available in 429 languages, the New Testament in 1,144 and at least one book of the Bible in 2,426 (www.biblesociety.org/index2.htm, 13 Mar 2008)

Spirit and the unity of the Body of Christ, but is especially seen in our renunciation of anti-Semitism. As increasing numbers begin to pray for the people and land of Israel, the church is actively cooperating with the spirit of Elijah.

The Holy Spirit had long before predicted that Israel as a nation would reject Jesus as Messiah (Isa 53:1-3) and that the riches of God's grace would go to the whole world (Gen 12:3). Now we see His assurance of a resurrection for Israel:

> For if their rejection is the reconciliation of the world, what will their acceptance be but life from the dead? (Rom 11:15)

This can only come from the nation at last accepting Jesus. We therefore need to watch the land of Israel for a major or national revival, perhaps preceded by a figure like John the Baptist:

> ...and thus all Israel will be saved; just as it is written, 'THE DELIVERER WILL COME FROM ZION; HE WILL REMOVE ALL UNGODLINESS FROM JACOB' (Rom 11:26)

Daniel's 70th Week Revisited

We also see here the fulfillment of Daniel's prophecy of the 70th week. Gabriel tells Daniel that seventy weeks has been decreed for Israel and Jerusalem...

> ...to finish the transgression, to make an end of sin, to make atonement for iniquity, to bring in everlasting righteousness, to seal up vision and prophecy (lit. prophet), and to anoint the most holy place (Dan 9:24)

Look at how each of these promises was a specific answer to Daniel's prayer:

(i) 'to finish the transgression, to make an end of sin, to make atonement for iniquity'
Daniel had just been confessing:

> we have sinned, committed iniquity... Indeed, all of Israel has transgressed Your law (Dan 9:5 & 11)

Gabriel's answer is that Israel has yet to *finish the transgression* – they will continue to transgress until the end of the 70th week. However, as we saw earlier, Jesus' death on the cross was in the midst of this week and in that single awe-inspiring sacrifice, He alone was able to *make an end of sin and atonement for iniquity* for all who believe (Heb 7:27). What is yet needed is for Israel to trust Him for that.

(ii) 'to bring in everlasting righteousness'
Daniel had prayed:

> Righteousness belongs to You, O Lord, but to us open shame (Dan 9:7)

Gabriel's promise is that Messiah will bring in everlasting righteousness for us and thus remove our shame (cf. 2 Cor 5:21)

(iii) 'to seal up vision and prophecy' [or, prophet]
Daniel had been confessing:

> Moreover, we have not listened to Your servants the prophets (Dan 9:6)

Gabriel's response again is that there is still a way to go, that the revelations of vision and prophet will continue to be sealed up as mysteries until the end of the 70th week. Any disciple of Jesus can understand these mysteries, as we have seen, but no one else will until the predicted events take place (Matt 13:10-17).

(iv) 'and to anoint the most holy place'
Lastly, Daniel had been pleading with God:

> Let now Your anger and Your wrath turn away from Your city Jerusalem… let Your face shine on Your desolate sanctuary (Dan 9:16-17)

Gabriel's promise, therefore, is that 'the most holy place' will be reconsecrated, as it was in the middle of this 70th week by Jesus 'in heaven itself' (Heb 9:23-24) for all who trust in Him. However, Gabriel then went on to warn that the rebuilt 'city and sanctuary' would be destroyed again as further 'desolations are determined', as seen in 70 AD We see therefore these desolations did take place in the 70th Week, as illustrated in Figure 3:

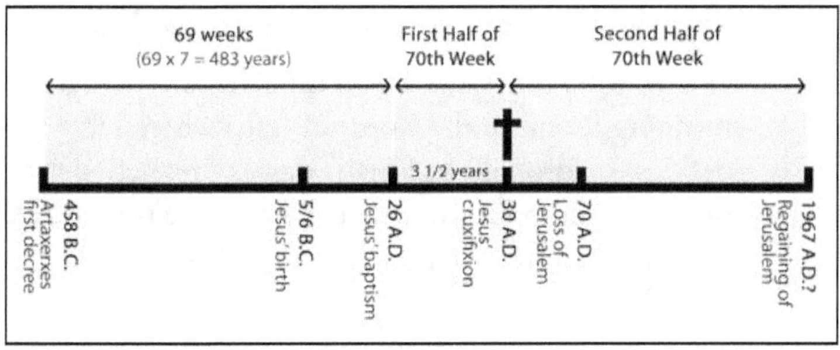

Figure 3 — Timeline of Daniel's 70 weeks

So now, at the end of the 70th week, as Israel softens and begins to believe in Him, these three associated mysteries of 'Elijah's coming', 'the times of the Gentiles' and 'the partial hardening of Israel' come to an end. At last, the woman is coming out of the wilderness.

Summary of This Era

(i) The dragon's failure to stop the coming of the woman's child, Messiah, resulted in his being thrown down from heaven so he turns again on the woman. This on-going hatred by the dragon and his angels reveals the demonic inspiration behind anti-Semitism, hatred of women and hatred of Christians.

(ii) God's grace is still extended to Israel despite her rejection of Jesus in 30 AD. She is 'nourished' and kept alive but she has to return to the wilderness, 'the wilderness of the nations.' This is a part of her redemption for she is given the great eagle's wings to get there and although still attacked by the dragon, she receives help from the earth.

(iii) Her time in the wilderness is for 'a time and times and half a time.' This description of three and a half years is the second half of Daniel's 70th week, the first half being the ministry of Jesus to Israel.

(iv) 'A time, times and half a time' has a typological meaning found in the words of Jesus where He defines the drought of Elijah's day as precisely that duration and points out that this was the time when God ignored the needs of Israel and helped Gentiles.

(v) This understanding is confirmed again in the words of Jesus after His resurrection when He commands His Jewish disciples to now 'make disciples of all the nations' (or, Gentiles). He also taught about 'the times of the Gentiles', predicting that Jerusalem would be 'trampled underfoot by the Gentiles until the times of the Gentiles are fulfilled.'

Literally, Jerusalem was 'trampled' by Gentiles until 1967, although the Temple Mount's status may also be a factor to consider.

(vi) The apostle John described this period of Gentile domination as 'forty two months', or three and a half years. The 'times of the Gentiles' are therefore prophetically or symbolically, 'a time and times and half a time' and literally or historically about two thousand years.

(vii) We cannot be dogmatic about precise historical dates, even 1967, because of the Temple Mount. We have, however, good reason to consider the 'season' because the fig tree, Israel, is clearly blossoming.

(viii) The original 'three years and six months' drought in Israel began and ended through the ministry of Elijah. Four hundred years later, Malachi, the last prophet of the Old Testament, predicted Elijah would come before Messiah and thus began the mystery of Elijah's return. Again, we find in the words of Jesus that just as Messiah has to come twice, Elijah does too.

(ix) Jesus tells us that John the Baptist was the first fulfillment, going forth in 'the spirit and power of Elijah', but that Elijah has still yet to come. These two spiritual comings of Elijah are separated by 'a time and times and half a time', or 'the times of the Gentiles', and mark the beginning and the end of the spiritual drought in Israel.

(x) This spiritual drought in Israel is called 'the mystery of the partial hardening of Israel' and when it ends, the latter rain of the Holy Spirit will water the ground and 'the earth will produce its fruit'. Paul adds that an indication of this time having arrived will be that 'the fullness of the Gentiles' will have 'come in' to the Kingdom of God. This is confirmed by Jesus' prediction that 'this gospel of the kingdom shall be preached in the whole world as a testimony to all the nations, and then the end will come' (Matt 24:14).

(xi) At the end of 'the times of the Gentiles', God brings the woman out of 'the wilderness of the nations' and back to the land of Israel, also restoring its fruitfulness, her language and her holy city and, eventually, 'the rain' of the Holy Spirit and the revelation of her Son and Messiah:

> And I will pour out on the house of David and on the inhabitants of Jerusalem, the Spirit of grace and of supplication, so that they will look on Me whom they have pierced;
> and they will mourn for Him, as one mourns for an only son, and they will weep bitterly over Him, like the bitter weeping over a first-born. (Zech 12:10)

(xii) The dragon, having failed to stop Messiah's birth and to destroy the woman, then turned to 'the rest of her offspring', which we are, if we 'keep the commandments of God and hold to the testimony of Jesus'.

(xiii) We find that God has faithfully answered every single detail of Daniel's prayers in Daniel, chapter 9.

11. What's Next?

We have seen here five distinct revelations, five unlocked mysteries, which perfectly dove-tail. The first is the woman or the mystery of Israel's survival, her continuing existence despite all the attempts of successive, powerful and ruthless Gentile empires to assimilate or annihilate her. Her reason for being was to bring forth the Child, the Lord Himself in human form, and despite her failings, God has never given up on her.

The second mystery is the dragon, the spirit behind the very different successive Gentile empires which have ruled over Israel and which each at some stage almost prevented the birth of Messiah. We identified the first six and in the next study will identify the seventh with its ten heads. The fact that Israel as a nation has yet to face the dragon's seventh head with its ten horns establishes beyond doubt that Israel's re-emergence onto the world stage in our time is hugely significant.

The third mystery is the time period, 'a time, times and half a time', which we found to be 'the times of the Gentiles', when God would help Gentiles more than the Jews, and was to end with the Jews regaining the city of Jerusalem. This time is determined by the fourth mystery, certainly the most recognised of the five in modern-day Judaism, the coming of Elijah and his effect on the nation of Israel, which we found requires two fulfillments to start and stop the drought of the Spirit on Israel.

This in turn introduces the fifth mystery, the 'partial hardening' of Israel – why the woman has been unable to accept her own Son.

Now, having established the real-time meaning of the metaphorical 'a time, times and half a time' as describing the last two thousand years, we have a key to unlock several more visions of Revelation and the next book in this series will examine chapter 13, the rise of the spirit of Antichrist.

Appendix A: Which Israel?

From the very beginning, there were two entities named 'Israel.' They were named after the man, Israel, formerly known as Jacob, son of Isaac and grandson of Abraham. Just as with other Biblical terms like 'flesh', 'head', 'angel' or 'generation', we have to examine the context to establish exactly which meaning of 'Israel' is intended where. Paul warns us that we need to understand this:

> For they are not all Israel who are descended from Israel (Rom 9:6)

He quotes Isaiah's description of them as the remnant:[129]

> And Isaiah cries out concerning Israel, THOUGH THE NUMBER OF THE SONS OF ISRAEL BE AS THE SAND OF THE SEA, IT IS THE REMNANT THAT WILL BE SAVED (Rom 9:27)

Isaiah is unambiguous – 'It is the remnant that will be saved.' Paul is likewise, that only those, whether Jew or Gentile, who have faith in Jesus as Messiah 'will be saved' (Rom 10:9-10). In this context, clearly only believers make up 'Israel'.

However, the Scriptures also use the name 'Israel' with another meaning altogether as is readily seen in Romans, chapters 9-11, where Paul uses both concepts. He begins his train of thought writing of his unceasing grief at Israel's unbelief:

> For I could wish that I myself was accursed, separated from Christ for the sake of my brethren, my kinsmen according to the flesh, who are Israelis, to whom belongs the adoption as sons and the glory and the covenants and the giving of the Law and the temple service and

---

[129] Isa 10:22

the promises, whose are the fathers, and from whom is the Messiah according to the flesh, who is over all, God blessed forever. Amen. (Rom 9:3-5)

Notice, Paul sees individual Israelis as belonging, 'according to the flesh', to a legitimate national entity. Jesus also came from this entity, 'according to the flesh'. However, in wishing he could take their place, Paul recognises them as 'accursed' and 'separated from Christ.' He goes on:

… but Israel, pursuing a law of righteousness, did not arrive at that law… because they did not pursue it by faith. (Rom 9:31-32)

In chapter 10, having taught in great detail on faith, he concludes again from Isaiah 65:2:

But as for Israel He says, ALL THE DAY LONG I HAVE STRETCHED OUT MY HANDS TO A DISOBEDIENT AND OBSTINATE PEOPLE (Rom 10:21)

And again, soon after:

That which Israel is seeking for, it has not obtained (Rom 11:7)

'Israel' in these three contexts refers to a people unequivocally in unbelief at the time Paul was writing. This was at least twenty years after Christ so it cannot be said that 'Israel' only refers to the believing remnant. We therefore have to accept both uses of the name 'Israel'.

Later in the Book of Revelation, we find John similarly referring to Jerusalem in both senses, as old and new Jerusalem, natural and spiritual, and it is essential for correct understanding that both uses of that name are also understood and accepted.

Appendix B: Hitler and the Churches

There has been much dispute about Hitler's Catholic faith. The following quotations, when considered in chronological order, show either his changing convictions or the unveiling of his duplicity as he promised at first, in April 1933, to protect the Catholic Church:

> 'I am personally convinced of the great power and deep significance of Christianity, and I won't allow any other religion to be promoted. That is why I have turned away from Ludendorff and that is why I reject the book by Rosenberg. It was written by a Protestant. It is not a Party book. It was not written by a Party man. The Protestants can be left to argue with him... As a Catholic, I never feel comfortable in the Evangelical Church or its structures... you can be sure: I will protect the rights and freedoms of the churches and not let them be touched, so that you need have no fears about the future of the Church.'[130]

Hitler's architect, Albert Speer, was a member of his inner circle and so was often an eye-witness of what happened behind the scenes. In his extraordinary memoirs, *Inside The Third Reich*, Speer also records Hitler's private denunciation of Rosenberg and Himmler's attempts to mythologise the SS, calling it 'a relapse into medieval notions'.[131]

In 1937, Hitler spoke publicly of an impersonal 'Almighty Providence':

---

[130] Hitler to Bishop Berning of Osnabruck, quoted by Burleigh, 2006, p. 174

[131] Speer, 1970, p. 143

'As weak as the individual may ultimately be in his character and actions as a whole, when compared to Almighty Providence and its will, he becomes just as infinitely strong the instant he acts in accordance with this Providence. Then there will rain down upon him the power that has distinguished all great phenomena in this world. And when I look back on the five years behind us, I cannot help but say: this has not been the work of man alone. Had Providence not guided us, I surely would often have been unable to follow these dizzying paths. That is something our critics should above all know. At the bottom of our hearts, we National Socialists are devout! We have no choice: no one can make national or world history if his deeds and abilities are not blessed by Providence.'[132]

He insisted on remaining in the Catholic Church. Speer again:

Around 1937, when Hitler heard that at the instigation of the party and the SS vast numbers of his followers had left the church because it was obstinately opposing his plans, he nevertheless ordered his chief associates, above all Goering and Goebbels, to remain members of the church. He too would remain a member of the Catholic Church, he said, although he had no real attachment to it. And in fact he remained in the church until his suicide.[133]

He also looked for ways to use the Protestants:

Amid his political associates in Berlin, Hitler made harsh pronouncements against the church, but in the

---

[132] Wurzberg, 27 June 1937. Domarus (ed.), *Hitler, Speeches And Proclamations 2*, p. 908. quoted by Burleigh, pp. 102-3
[133] Speer, 1970, p. 142

presence of women he adopted a milder tone... 'The church is certainly necessary for the people. It is a strong and conservative element', he might say at one time or another in this private circle [tea-time talks at his home at Obersalzberg]. However, he conceived of the church as an instrument that could be useful to him. 'If only Reibi (this was his nickname for Reich Bishop Ludwig Muller) had some kind of stature. But why do they appoint a nobody of an army chaplain? I'd be glad to give him my full support. Think of all he could do with that. Through me the Evangelical (Protestant) Church could become the established church, as in England.'[134]

This did not stop him condemning many Christian individuals or groups who disagreed with him. In 1937, in a fit of rage at 'a rebellious sermon' by Pastor Martin Niemoller, Hitler ordered Niemoller's permanent incarceration in a concentration camp.

However, until 1942:

> Hitler went on maintaining that he regarded the church as indispensable in political life... He sharply condemned the campaign against the church, calling it a crime against the future of the nation. For it was impossible, he said, to replace the church by any 'party ideology'. Undoubtedly, he continued, the church would learn to adapt to the political goals of National Socialism in the long run, as it had always adapted in the course of history.[135]

He showed no interest in Jesus and true spirituality but only in institutions as a means of control:

[134] Speer, 1970, p. 141
[135] Ibid., p. 142

Hitler was impressed by the organisation and power of the [Catholic] Church. Its hierarchical structure, its skill in dealing with human nature and the unalterable nature of its Creed, were all features from which he claimed to have learned. For the Protestant clergy he felt only contempt: '…they have neither a religion nor a great position to defend like Rome'. It was the 'great position' of the Church that he respected, the fact that it lasted for so many centuries; towards its teaching he showed the sharpest hostility. In Hitler's eyes Christianity was a religion fit only for slaves; he detested its ethics in particular. Its teaching, he declared, was a rebellion against the natural law of selection by struggle and the survival of the fittest. 'Taken to its logical extreme, Christianity would mean the systematic cultivation of human failure.'[136]

He actually preferred Islam:

Hitler had been much impressed by a scrap of history he had learned from a delegation of distinguished Arabs. When the Mohammedans attempted to penetrate beyond France into Central Europe during the eighth century, his visitors had told him, they had been driven back at the Battle of Tours. Had the Arabs won this battle, the world would be Mohammedan today. For theirs was a religion that believed in spreading the faith by the sword and subjugating all nations to that faith. The Germanic peoples would have become heirs to that faith. Such a creed was perfectly suited to the Germanic temperament. Hitler said that the conquering Arabs, because of their racial inferiority, would in the long run have been unable to

[136] Alan Bullock, *Hitler: a Study in Tyranny*, Penguin, Revised edition 1962, p. 388. References given as a conversation with Rauschning on 7 April 1933 and Hitler's *Table Talk*.

contend with the harsher climate and conditions of the country. They could not have kept down the more vigorous natives, so that ultimately not Arabs but Islamicised Germans could have stood at the head of this Mohammedan empire.

Hitler usually concluded this historical speculation by remarking: 'You see, it's been our misfortune to have the wrong religion. Why didn't we have the religion of the Japanese, who regard sacrifice for the Fatherland as the highest good? The Mohammedan religion too would have been much more compatible to us than Christianity. Why did it have to be Christianity with its meekness and flabbiness?'[137]

By late 1942, Hitler was telling his inner circle that the gloves were coming off:

'I'll make these damn parsons feel the power of the State in a way they would never have dreamed possible! For the moment I am just keeping my eye on them; if I ever have the slightest suspicion that they are getting dangerous, I will shoot the lot of them. This filthy reptile raises its head wherever there is a sign of weakness in the State and therefore it must be stamped on whenever it does. The fate of a few filthy, lousy Jews and epileptics is not worth bothering about. The foulest of the carrion are those who come clothed in the cloak of humility... The Catholic Church has but one desire, and that is to see us destroyed.'[138]

[137] Speer, 1970, pp. 142-143
[138] *Hitler's Table Talk,* 11 Aug 1942, pp. 625-6; quoted by Burleigh, p. 102

          Dancing in the Dragon's Jaws

Perhaps the final comment should be left to Albert Einstein, himself a German Jew. In late 1940, he said:

> Only the church stood squarely across the path of Hitler's campaign for suppressing the truth. I had never any special interest in the church before, but now I feel a great admiration because the church alone has had the courage and persistence to stand for intellectual truth and moral freedom. I am forced thus to confess that what I once despised, I now praise unreservedly.[139]

[139] *Time* interview, 'German Martyrs', 23 Dec 1940, p. 38. Quoted by Michael Burleigh, p. 213, *Sacred Causes (Religion and Politics From European Dictators To Al-Qaeda)*, HarperPress 2006.

Appendix C: Dating Daniel's 70th Week

Sir Robert Anderson (1841-1918), Chief of the Criminal Investigation Department of Scotland Yard, made a widely-accepted argument for Artaxerxes' second decree as being issued on 14 March, 445 BC and that this prophecy was fulfilled on 6 April, 32 AD when Jesus made His triumphant entrance to Jerusalem before His crucifixion. Although this would make the time elapsed 478 years, rather than the predicted 483 years, Sir Robert recalculated this period as 173,880 days or 483 lunar years, allowing for intercalation (the insertion of leap years). He also interpreted 'until Messiah the Prince' (Dan 9:25) as not being fulfilled until Jesus entered Jerusalem mounted on a donkey, to also fulfill Zechariah 9:9, 'Behold, your King…'.

It is further argued that of the four decrees, only Artaxerxes' second aimed to 'restore and rebuild Jerusalem', including 'with plaza (or, streets) and moat' (Dan 9:25), whereas the other three decrees specified only the temple.

There are several problems with this view. Firstly, in regard to the four decrees, Isaiah predicted that God would use Cyrus to decree and begin this restoration:

> Thus says the LORD, 'It is I who says of Cyrus, 'He is My shepherd!'
> And he will perform all My desire; even declaring of Jerusalem, 'She shall be built',
> And of the temple, 'Your foundation will be laid' (Isa 44:28)

This means that as God sees it, Cyrus's decree was to rebuild Jerusalem and included the temple. Isaiah prophesied again:

'I have aroused him in righteousness, and I will make all
his ways smooth;
He will build My city, and will let My exiles go free,
without any payment or reward' (Isa 45:13)

We cannot, therefore, rule out any of the four decrees on the grounds of Daniel 9:25 being strictly limited to 'restore and rebuild Jerusalem'. All four qualify.

As for Sir Robert's interpretation of 'until Messiah the Prince' meaning Jesus' triumphant entry into Jerusalem, this was not actually the first or only time Jesus was proclaimed as Messiah or Prince. Mary was told of His true identity before He was conceived (Luke 1:26-35), as was Joseph soon after (Matt 1:20-21) and Elizabeth (Luke 1:41-45). Some shepherds were told at His birth (Luke 2:8-14), Simeon and Anna were told forty days after His birth (Luke 2:25-38) and even King Herod was told by the Magi (Matt 2:1ff).

However, the first public declaration was when Jesus went to John to be baptized, when He left His work as a carpenter to begin His public ministry as Messiah the Prince. 'Messiah' means 'the Anointed One' and at His baptism He was anointed with a visible manifestation of the Holy Spirit while the Father announced it out loud from heaven (Matt 3:16-17, John 1:29-34).

This occurred in about 26 AD, which is 483 years from Artaxerxes' first decree in 458 BC.[140]

---

[140] *Zondervan's Pictorial Encyclopedia of the Bible, Vol.1*, p. 340. For more details regarding this date, see the earlier section, there being no year zero between BC and AD.

Appendix D: 'Why Should the Jews Have the Land?'

There is good reason for Israel's presence in the land but it is not because Jews are better than Palestinians. When God was about to bring them out of Babylon some 500 years BC, He was explicit:

> 'It is not for your sake, O house of Israel, that I am about to act, but for My holy name, which you have profaned among the nations where you went. I will vindicate the holiness of My great name which has been profaned among the nations, which you have profaned in their midst… For I will take you from the nations, gather you from all the lands and bring you into your own land' (Ezek 36:22-24)

God acted then because *He had decided* to do so, *despite* Israel's profanities, but also because He foresaw how they would respond:

> '… you shall remember your own evil ways, and your doings that were not good, and shall despise yourselves in your own sight for your iniquities and for your abominations. I do not do this for your sake', says the Lord GOD, 'be it known to you. Be ashamed and confounded for your ways, O house of Israel!' (Ezek 36:31-32)

He regathered the nation of Israel, knowing they would become ashamed of their own ways. It was also to reveal Himself to every other nation as well:

> 'Then the nations will know that I am the LORD,' declares the Lord GOD, 'when I prove Myself holy among you in

> their sight. For I will take you from the nations, gather
> you from all the lands and bring you into your own land.
> Then I will sprinkle clean water on you, and you will be
> clean; I will cleanse you from all your filthiness and from
> all your idols…' (Ezek 36:23b-25)

Notice it was to Israel's own land and before they had repented.

This meant the regathering happened centre-stage, 'in the midst of the earth among the people' (Isa 24:13), i.e. at the junction of three continents (Asia, Europe and Africa), so that the whole earth could see and acknowledge what He had done. This was true of Israel's return from Babylon and, as we will see, it is also true of their return from 'all the nations' in our time.

Is This the Time?

Seeing the present ungodliness of Israel, some teach today that Israel must have regained the land by illegitimate means, that this regathering is not of God but of their own ungodly efforts. For example, Art Katz, a prophetic Messianic Jew, taught that God will scatter Israel again to demonstrate this before He gathers them again in His own way.[141]

Others teach that there is nothing in the New Testament to promise the Jews anything at all unless they turn to Jesus as their Messiah so that no time can be right for the land. However, this teaching overlooks several passages which are explained away by a popular misunderstanding that they

---

[141] *The Holocaust – Where Was God?*, p. 85 and http://
www.benisrael.org/site_content/principalburdens/
frmst_principalburdens.htm, 8 May, 2007

refer to a time after the Second Coming, rather than before. One passage requires no prior correction of interpretation:

> ... they will fall by the edge of the sword, and will be led captive into all the nations; and Jerusalem will be trampled under foot by the Gentiles *until* the times of the Gentiles are fulfilled (Luke 21:24 emphasis added)

From the plain, unambiguous words of Jesus, if Jerusalem was to be held by non-Jews for a finite time, the times of the Gentiles, then the Jews have to get it back at the end of that time. Otherwise, the word 'until' has no meaning.

As to when that time is, this book shows how the 'times of the Gentiles' may now be being fulfilled.

Lastly, at the present time, when one third of the nations of the earth are Islamic, remember Israel's location – in the very centre of the Islamic empire which is calling for her annihilation. We will consider this further in the next book in this series.

Appendix E: 'But What of the Palestinians Today?'

We cannot ignore this cry of the heart. God has no favourites (Rom 10:12) so He surely loves Palestinian Arabs as much as He loves Jews. However, Israel's return to the land has hugely impacted the Palestinians, as documented by their eloquent and gracious countrymen such as Edward Said, Naim Ateek, Alex Awad and Elias Chacour as well as by Western journalists such as Robert Fisk, John Pilger and Gywnne Dyer, and world-renowned Jewish intellectual Noam Chomsky.[142]

Our daily newspapers and nightly television news programmes often feature gut-wrenching accounts of the hardships faced by the Palestinians, caused by their displacement into refugee camps when the state of Israel emerged. The privations of these camps are then said to be the primary cause of Palestinian militancy and suicide bombings.

Most Palestinian advocates make no claim to be Christian but Naim Ateek and Alex Awad do, appealing to

---

[142] For example, Edward Said's *The Question of Palestine* (London: Vintage, 1992); Naim Ateek's essays *Biblical Perspectives On The Land* and *A Palestinian Perspective: The Bible And Liberation*, in *Voices From The Margin* (ed. R.S. Sugirtharajah, New York: Orbis, 1995); Alex Awad's *Through The Eyes of The Victims*, (Bethlehem Bible College, 2001); Elias Chacour's *Blood Brothers (A Palestinian's Struggle For Reconciliation In The Middle East)* (E. Sussex: Kingsway, 1986); Robert Fisk's *The Great War For Civilisation: The Conquest Of The Middle East* (London: Harper Collins, 2005); Noam Chomsky's *The Fateful Triangle: The United States, Israel And Palestine* (Boston: South End Press, updated 1999)

---

the Scriptures for solutions, as does Elias Chacour in his powerful book *Blood Brothers* citing his father's words:

> '…the Jews and Palestinians are brothers – blood brothers. We share the same father, Abraham, and the same God. We must never forget that. Now we get rid of the gun.'[143]

I therefore stand with many Palestinian brothers and sisters in Christ who have got rid of the gun. However, I also want to rightly understand the Scriptures to know God's will in it all and to ask some questions that need answering by wiser heads than mine.

Let me begin, then, with my personal grief at the Palestinians' plight. They are in a nightmarish situation, crushed between Israel's desperate fight for survival and the ambitions of pan-Arabists and Islamists (to be considered in the next study in this series). Despite Israel's desperation, there is no excuse for any injustice that any Israeli commits against any Palestinian. Every one of us will face:

> the righteous judgment of God, who will render to each person according to his deeds… There will be tribulation and distress for every soul of man who does evil, of the Jew first and also of the Greek, but glory and honor and peace to everyone who does good, to the Jew first and also to the Greek; for there is no partiality with God (Rom 2:5-11)

This is unequivocal. God will righteously judge every Jew for his sins before He judges any Palestinian for his sins – the Jews have priority in facing His judgment as well as in

---

[143] Elias Chacour, *Blood Brothers (A Palestinian's Struggle For Reconciliation In The Middle East)* E. Sussex: Kingsway, 1986, p. 34

possessing the land. There is no doubt that every Jewish participant in the 1948 Deir Yassin massacre – in which an estimated 110 men, women and children were killed[144] – will be held accountable on that day. This and other alleged Jewish atrocities[145] are often examined by Jews of conscience such as Benny Morris, or Ari Folman in his award winning movie, *Waltz With Bashir*. Even Robert Fisk acknowledges:

> But if Israeli historians have proved the truth of this, Arab historians have remained largely silent about their own side's iniquities in this [1948] and other wars.[146]

Some of the worst atrocities against Palestinians have actually been committed by fellow Arabs, yet Israel alone is condemned. Remember the 1972 massacre of eleven Israeli athletes in Munich? It was carried out by Black September, an organisation named for September 1970. At that time, the Arabs of the *Jordanian* army killed three thousand Palestinians in a civil war when the PLO tried, with Syrian help, to overthrow Hashemite rule. In 1982, in the Lebanese refugee camps of Sabra and Chatila and the aftermath, an estimated 1,700 men, woman and children[147] were shot in cold blood by Arab Phalangists, Maronite Christian allies of Israel. An Israeli commission of inquiry held their Defence Minister, Ariel Sharon, personally responsible for not preventing this but there is no doubt that the massacre was

---

[144] Uri Milstein, www.hirhome.com/israel/milstein-deir-yassin.htm, 23 Mar 2011
[145] http://www.soundofegypt.com/palestinian/adult/massacres.htm#YASIN, 17 Apr, 2009
[146] *The Great War for Civilisation: the Conquest of the Middle East*, p. 462
[147] Ibid., p. 1026

perpetrated by the Lebanese, taking the opportunity to remove Palestinians from Lebanon. Mr Fisk goes on to record that 300 of these victims were killed three weeks later in what became a Lebanese army base.

That accepted, exactly what issues need to be addressed?

(i) Who is a 'Palestinian'?

Just as we had to ask 'Who is Israel?' and 'Who is a Jew?', we have to ask 'Who is a Palestinian?'

For example, what should we make of there never having been a nation-state called Palestine? Calls for its creation only began last century when Israel's rebirth became a possibility. In 135 AD the Roman emperor Hadrian renamed the land of Israel 'Provincia Syria Palaestina' to obliterate all trace of the Jews after seemingly endless rebellions there. For the next one and a half thousand years, the land remained a province of the Byzantine, Arab Islamic and Ottoman Empires, right up until the end of World War I when the League of Nations created the British Mandate of Palestine. The British Mandate of Palestine lasted from 1920 to 1948 and at that time, all inhabitants of the area, Jews included, were called Palestinians. For example, in World War II, the 'Palestine Regiment' consisted of three Jewish battalions and one Arab.

The division of the mandated area called Palestine began in 1921 when the British handed over 77% to the Hashemite dynasty who had been displaced as guardians of Mecca and Medina by the House of Saud. This area, initially called Transjordan or Transjordania (i.e. all the land 'across the Jordan', from the east bank of the Jordan River to Iraq and Saudi Arabia), became today's 'Hashemite Kingdom of Jordan.'

However, changing the name does not change the ethnicity of the people. It is generally accepted that 60% of Jordan's population are Palestinian Arabs but this presumes that all those living in the Palestinian Mandate east of the Jordan in 1947 are first redefined as *not* being Palestinians, as conceded in July, 2010, by Robert Fisk in his article, *Why Jordan is Occupied by Palestinians:*

> The term Palestinian broadly refers to Arabs who declined Israeli citizenship in 1948, when the country was formed. Previously, it had referred to the occupants of the territories controlled by Britain, including modern Israel.[148]

Notice, his first definition refers only to West Bank Arabs and excludes those from the East Bank. If, however, we do not backdate the 1948 definition to 1947, the Palestinian population of Jordan may be as high as 80% to 85%. In the same article, Fisk reported some of the Jordanian king's advisers, former General Ali Habashneh, Colonel Beni Sahar and Major General Mohamed Jamal Majalli, as complaining that:

> …by 1988, 1.95 million Palestinians held Jordanian citizenship. Another 850,000 hold citizenship that the ex-army men [in July 2010] regard as illegal. Another 950,000 Palestinians from the West Bank live legally, but without citizenship, on the East Bank – in other words, in Jordan. Another 300,000 come from Gaza. The ex-army officers see a 'silent transfer' of Palestinians across the Jordan river.

---

[148] www.independent.co.uk/opinion/commentators/fisk/robert-fisk-why-jordan-is-occupied-by-palestinians-2032173.html, 23 Mar, 2011

This means they recognise at least 4.05 million Palestinians in their total population of 6.113 million (i.e. 66%) but if population growth is included since 1988, that figure may be as high as 94%.[149]

Until 1988, both Palestinian and Jordanian leaders used to proclaim, 'Jordan is Palestine and Palestine is Jordan' (for more details, see Appendix F).

Listen, for example, to Anwar al-Khatib, former mayor of East Jerusalem, speaking in 1986: 'Palestine, Jordan and Syria constituted one family until the British and French occupation in 1918, which drove the wedge of boundaries among us. We do not differentiate between our people, whether they live in Jordan, Syria, or Palestine'.[150] It may therefore be incorrect to speak today of the West Bank as 'occupied' by Israel since it was Jordanian territory in 1967 and Jordan formally renounced ownership in 1988.

(ii) What of the events of 1921-22?

I have asked advocates for the Palestinian cause their view of the events of 1921-22, only to be told they did not concern themselves with anything prior to 1948. Why not?

---

[149] www.dos.gov.jo/sdb_pop/sdb_pop_e/ehsaat/alsokan/2010/2-1.pdf, 24 Mar, 2011. A University of Jordan study records that Jordan's population grew from 1988-1995 at a rate of 3.4% [www.aaas.org/international/ehn/waterpop/jordan.htm, 23 Mar, 2011] and the Jordanian Department of Statistics show that slowing from 1999 (2.5%) to 2010 (2.2%). They give no figures for 1996 to 1998 but assuming the lower figure of 2.5%, the original 1.95 million Palestinians with Jordanian citizenship would seem to have grown to about 3.65 million by 2010. With the advisers' estimates of another 2.1 million as either "illegals", residents or refugees from Gaza, this would today mean some 5.75 million Palestinians out of the 6,113,000 or 94%.

[150] http://www.danielpipes.org/article/298, 11 May, 2007

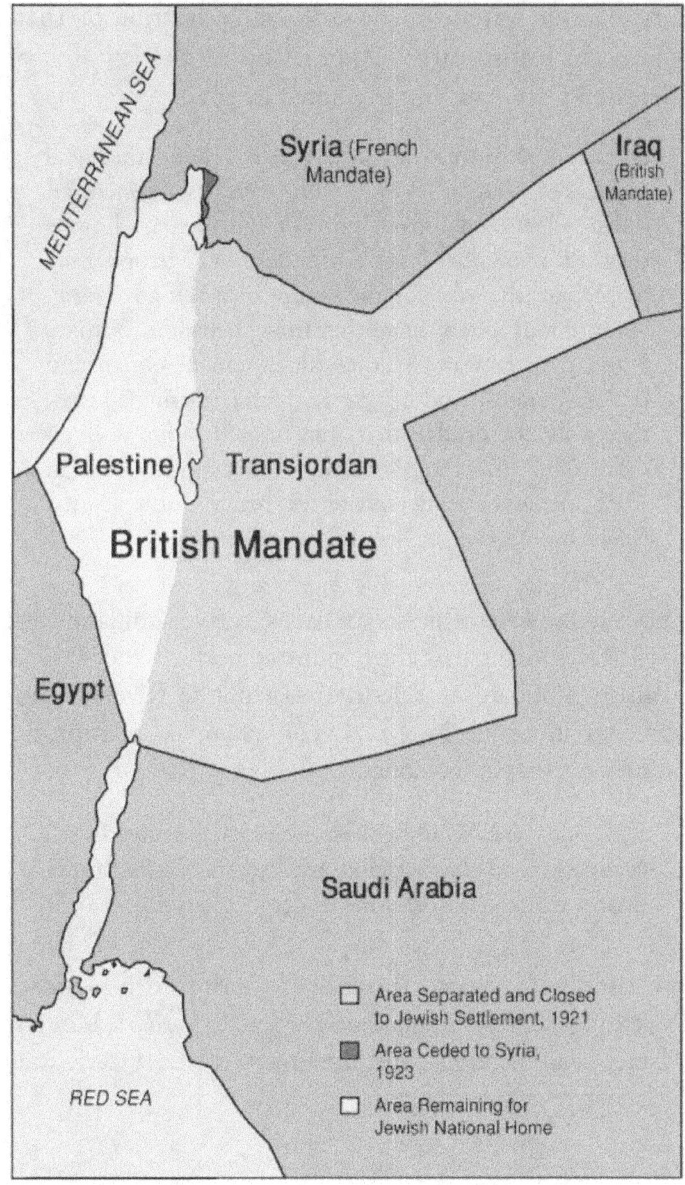

Figure (iv) Great Britain's Division of the Mandated Area 1921–1923
source: www.jewishvirtuallibrary.org/jsource/images/maps/mandate2.gif

Lord Balfour, author of the Balfour Declaration of 1917 by which the British carved a homeland for the Jews out of the defeated Ottoman Empire, noted in 1920:

> So far as the Arabs are concerned, I hope they will remember that it is we who have established an independent Arab sovereignty of the Hedjaz. I hope they will remember it is we who desire in Mesopotamia to prepare the way for the future of a self-governing, autonomous Arab State [creating Lebanon, Jordan, Syria, Iraq, Kuwait, Saudi Arabia, Yemen, Oman and the Gulf States], and I hope that, remembering all that, they will not grudge that small notch – for it is no more than that geographically – that small notch in what are now Arab territories being given to the [Jews].[151]

Is it not unjust, when Palestinian Arabs today claim land west of the River Jordan, that they count as nothing the 77% of the British Mandate of Palestine, east of the River Jordan, which they received in 1921? For example, high-profile advocate Robert Fisk has concluded:

> '...in 1967 the West Bank and Gaza fell under Israeli occupation, so that Israel at last had the entire former British mandate of Palestine under its control.'[152]

This is simply incorrect. 'The entire former British mandate of Palestine' actually included *all the land of Jordan*. Modern day Israel has only ever controlled most of the 23% left, as Fisk elsewhere acknowledges:

---

[151] Sir Martin Gilbert, *The Routledge Atlas of the Arab-Israeli Conflict,* 7th Edition, London, 2002, p. 7
[152] Fisk, p. 463

The Palestinians wanted a state, even if it was built on
less than 22% of mandate Palestine [emphasis added] [153]

Yet Fisk makes no comment on the creation or composition of Jordan. Why is this division of the land left out of the equation for peace? If the 'one family' of 'Palestine, Jordan and Syria' has disagreements amongst themselves as to who controls which area of all the lands they possess, why should that count against Israel?

This is often overlooked even by Christian leaders. The legendary Brother Andrew, *God's Smuggler* and founder of Open Doors, has poured his life into reconciliation; his book, *Light Force: the Only Hope for the Middle East*, passionately urges the people of God to be light in the darkness. Andrew is often misunderstood and even vilified for meeting and demonstrating his and God's love for Yasser Arafat and many of the leaders of Islamic Jihad and Hamas in Lebanon and Gaza for over fifteen years. Throughout this time, Andrew was and still is a Zionist. However, in his book's overview of the history of the Palestinian issues, even Andrew completely overlooks the creation of Jordan from 77% of Palestine.

(iii) Jordan's actions between 1948 and 1967

Jordan controlled the West Bank between 1948 and 1967. Some claim today that their 1948 invasion of the West Bank was to protect the Palestinians, Jordan's official website stating that in April 1950, the Jordanian Parliament 'unanimously approved a motion to unite the two banks of the Jordan River, constitutionally expanding the Hashemite Kingdom of Jordan in order to safeguard what was left of the Arab territory of Palestine from further Zionist

---

[153] Fisk, p. 1281

expansion.'[154] If this was so, why did Jordan not establish it as another autonomous Palestinian state when they had the opportunity? After all, they ruled the West Bank for almost twenty years. Why did they instead attempt to annex it? The answer is found in Appendix F: *'Jordan is Palestine and Palestine is Jordan'*.

(iv) Who are the refugees?

In 1950, the official UN figure was 711,000 Palestinian Arabs[155] but this included those newly arrived in Israel or the Palestinian mandate as economic refugees from the Arab nations. The definition created by the United Nations' Works and Relief Agency (UNWRA) is actually unique to this situation: anyone 'whose normal place of residence was Palestine between June 1946 and May 1948.'[156] A better way to establish accurate figures is to note that before the 1948 War, the Arab population was 1.2 million and when the fighting stopped in 1949, between 450,000 and 550,000 were living in areas not controlled by Israel. This means between 650,000 and 750,000 had been living in Israeli-controlled areas. Since approximately 160,000 were still there or were allowed to return to their homes, we find that between 490,000 and 590,000 were displaced.[157]

The UN's figures were not helped by the huge incentive for fraud. By 1952, UNWRA estimated it was feeding approximately 1 million refugees and it is obviously impossible for the population to have grown by 50% in those two years. In 1959, a spot-check by a group of US senators of the registrations of 145 refugees revealed that 61 were fraudulent. In 1967's Six Day War, Israel gained control of

---

[154] http://www.kinghussein.gov.jo/his_palestine.html, 15 May, 2007

[155] In 2005, this was amended to 914,000 with 4.4 million descendants

[156] www.un.org/unrwa/refugees/whois.html, 10 Mar, 2008

[157] Terence Prittie, *The Palestinians*, Transaction Books, 1975, pp. 52-53

the Gaza Strip and, from UNWRA's figures, a population of 312,000 refugees and 118,000 original residents. However, the census found only 222,000 refugees but 134,000 residents.[158] Even if the Israelis were biased in removing the 16,000 residents off the refugee register, that still leaves UNWRA providing for 74,000 non-existent refugees.

After comparing many different sources and methods, the most consistently calculated and likely number of Arab or Palestinian refugees in 1948 is about 600,000.[159] As for their on-going plight, Robert Fisk says he has 'written at great length about the Palestinian dispossession of 1948… and the fate of the 750,000 Palestinian refugees and their millions of descendants today, many of whom rot in the squalor of camps in Lebanon, Syria, Jordan and occupied West Bank and Syria.'[160]

While that remains vital, why do we not hear at similarly 'great length' about the plight of the 856,000 Jewish refugees from the Arab nations at the same time? Does it mean nothing that they too had to leave their homes and livelihoods in Morocco (248,000), Iraq (150,000), Algeria (140,000), Tunisia (103,000), Egypt (63,500), Yemen (46,000), Libya (36,000), Syria (15,000), Lebanon, Aden and Iran, as well as 17,000 from the Arab areas of Palestine.[161] Although acknowledged as official U.N. figures,[162] it was 60 years, March 2008, before the United Nations Human

---

[158] Ibid., p. 56

[159] www.mideastweb.org/palpop.htm, 15 Nov 2007

[160] Fisk, p. 462

[161] http://www.justiceforjews.com/index.html, 12 May, 2008

[162] http://www.nytimes.com/2007/11/05/world/middleeast/05nations.html?
ex=1352005200&en=93fd256f53c21587&ei=5124&partner=permalin
k&exprod=permalink, 20 July, 2009

Rights Council finally heard the case.[163] In leaving Arab lands, these Jewish refugees left not only frozen bank accounts, homes, businesses and other assets but also an estimated 100,000 square kilometres of Jewish-owned land, or four times the size of the State of Israel.[164]

Of these Jewish refugees, an estimated 600,000 found refuge in Israel (their last tent city closing in 1958) and 250,000 in Europe and the Americas. All needed to be integrated into their new homelands without UN help, so why cannot the Palestinians be too, with UN help? Because they are not allowed to be. In 1949, the Arab League passed a resolution prohibiting any Arab nation from granting citizenship to Palestinian refugees. That this is still in effect can be seen in Saudi Arabia in 2004 – Palestinian refugees living there, and by then swollen to 500,000, were the only ex-patriates forbidden to become Saudi citizens 'to avoid dissolution of their identity and protect their right to return to their homeland.'[165] Indeed, of all the Arab nations, only Jordan has freely allowed Palestinians to become citizens.

(v) Why are we using different standards?

The 1937 Peel Commission on Palestine was roundly condemned for recommending that 'sooner or later there should be a transfer of land and, as far as possible, an exchange of population', estimated then as affecting '225,000 Arabs and 1,250 Jews' who would have to move. Their report noted that this transfer of population was considered to be the only possible solution in other spheres

---

[163] http://www.justiceforjews.com/geneva2008.html, 12 May, 2008

[164] http://www.justiceforjews.com/biblio-book.doc; also the World Organization of Jews from Arab Countries (WOJAC), http://wojac.com, 12 May, 2008

[165] www.asianews.it/index.php?art=1760&l=en, 10 Mar, 2008

of brutal antagonism. For example, at the same time as Transjordan was being split off from the British Mandate of Palestine, the Treaty of Lausanne (1923) required some two and a half million people to be formally denaturalised as 1.5 million Greeks and Christians were expelled from Turkish territory and 800,000 Turks and Muslims from Greek territory. In the 1947 partition of India, the only perceived solution to Muslim-Hindu warfare was for fourteen million people to change homelands, 7 million Muslims moving to East and West Pakistan from India and 7 million Hindus and Sikhs from Pakistan to India.

What if all these refugees had been treated as the Palestinians have been, ushered into camps along the borders, to be sustained by the United Nations? It is hard to avoid the conclusion that the whole situation of the Palestinian refugees has been cynically, brutally, created and maintained by those who do not accept Israel's right to exist as a nation.

Appendix F: 'Jordan is Palestine & Palestine is Jordan'?

The 1921 division of the land by the British was fiercely resented by the Palestinian Arabs. After the Palestinian Liberation Organisation (PLO) was formed in 1964, its first leader, Ahmad ash-Shuqayri, declared that Palestine "stretched from the Mediterranean Sea in the west to the Syrian-Iraqi desert".[166]

The founding PLO Charter was unequivocal:

> Article 2: Palestine, with its boundaries at the time of the British Mandate, is a [*sic*] indivisible territorial unit.

Nevertheless, the PLO accepted Jordan's claim to the West Bank:

> Article 24: This Organization does not exercise any territorial sovereignty over the West Bank in the Hashemite Kingdom of Jordan, on the Gaza Strip or in the Himmah Area. Its activities will be on the national popular level in the liberational, organizational, political and financial fields.[167]

On 23 November 1967, the PLO rejected the UN's Resolution 242, despite its calling on Israel to give back occupied territory, because 'it refers to Israel's right to exist

---

[166] www.danielpipes.org/article/298, 11 May, 2007, documented in *Greater Syria: the History of an Ambition*, Oxford University Press USA, 1992.
[167] www.mideastweb.org/palestinian_charter.htm, 23 Mar, 2011

and to establish permanent, recognised frontiers…'[168] Also, because 'it would strengthen the human and geographic barrier that separates the Arab homeland into east and west. This would be extremely injurious as it would prevent the achievement of even partial, not to mention total, Arab unity'.[169] Article 2 of that declaration reaffirmed that 'Palestine with its boundaries that existed at the time of the British mandate is an integral regional unit'.[170]

In 1971, the eighth conference of the Palestine National Council (PNC) resolved that 'what links Jordan to Palestine is a national bond and a national unity formed, since time immemorial, by history and culture. The establishment of one political entity in Transjordan and another in Palestine is illegal'.[171] This is why the Palestinians tried to take control of Jordan in 1970, aided by Syrian tanks, only to be defeated during 'Black September' and later take convoluted revenge by killing the Israeli athletes in Munich in 1972.

In June 1974, the Palestinian National Council's twelfth session resolved that:

> Article 5. The PLO will struggle with the Jordanian national forces for the establishment of a Jordanian-Palestinian national front whose aim is the establishment of a national democratic government in Jordan – a government that will cohere with the Palestinian entity to be established as a result of the struggle.[172]

[168] *The Israeli-Palestinian Conflict: A Documentary Record 1967-1990*, ed. Yehuda Lukacs, Cambridge University Press, 1991, p. 290

[169] Ibid., p. 299, PLO declaration, Section C, article 4

[170] Ibid., p. 292

[171] Published in Lebanese newspaper *al-Anwar*, 5 Mar, 1971, and Daniel Pipes as above.

[172] www.mideastweb.org/plo1974.htm, 21 July, 2010

The division of the land was also deeply resented by the Jordanians. Their first king, Abdullah, repeatedly stated, 'Palestine is one unit. The division between Palestine and Transjordan is artificial and wasteful'. From the establishment of the state of Israel in 1948, Jordan kept control of the West Bank, formally annexing it in 1950 until forced to back down by the other Arab nations. In 1959, their prime minister declared: 'We here in Jordan, led by our great [second] king [Hussein], are the government of Palestine, the army of Palestine, and we are the refugees'. In 1965, Hussein was unequivocal: 'the two peoples have integrated; Palestine has become Jordan and Jordan Palestine', adding that 'those organizations which seek to differentiate between Palestinians and Jordanians are traitors who help Zionism in its aim of splitting the Arab camp.... We have only one army, one political organization, and one popular recruiting system in this country'.[173]

In 1975, Jordanian Prime Minister Zayd ar-Rifa'I stated:

> Jordan is Palestine. They have never been ruled as two separate states except during the British Mandate. Before 1918 the two banks of the Jordan River were a single state. When they returned to being a single state after 1948, it was a matter of building on the earlier unity. Their families are one, as are their welfare, affiliation, and culture.[174]

In 1986, Anwar al-Khatib, former Jordanian mayor of East Jerusalem declared: 'Palestine, Jordan and Syria constituted one family until the British and French occupation in 1918, which drove the wedge of boundaries among us. We do not differentiate between our people, whether they live in

---

[173] www.danielpipes.org/article/298, 11 May, 2007, documented in *Greater Syria: the History of an Ambition*, Oxford University Press USA, 1992.
[174] Ibid.

                    Dancing in the Dragon's Jaws

Jordan, Syria, or Palestine.' I heard a similar sentiment expressed in Jerusalem in September 2008 when I asked a young Jordanian man what he called this area prior to the creation of Jordan. He replied, 'We called it counties of Damascus.' It was not until 31 July, 1988, that King Hussein changed Jordan's official stance, declaring: 'There should be the separation of the West Bank from the Hashemite Kingdom of Jordan.'

Polemicist Daniel Pipes publicises these statements by Palestinian and Jordanian leaders but does not himself accept the premise that 'Jordan is Palestine and Palestine is Jordan'. He summarises:

> Palestinians cast an occasional covetous glance toward the hinterland; this helps explain in part the Jordanian-PLO war of 1970. Their periodic claims to Husayn's kingdom also reflect an intent to bring down the Hashemites as a aid to conquering Palestine. For their part, Jordanians have cast frequent envious glances at the coastline; 'Abdallah spent long years plotting to establish a presence on the West Bank and his grandson Husayn, while more subtle and less driven, has also devoted many efforts to this end.
>
> Whenever Husayn declared that 'Jordan is Palestine and Palestine is Jordan,' he had at least three purposes. First, as Asher Susser observes, it was his way of asserting that 'Jordan deserves to play a central and decisive role in the determination of the political fate of the Palestinians.' Second, the king's remarks were aimed toward Palestinians under Israeli occupation, where the Hashemite-PLO battle for Palestinian favor rages hardest. Third, Hashemite statements have to be seen in the light of efforts to integrate and manage east bank Palestinians. The many Palestinians on the east bank, estimated between 40 and 70 percent of the total

population, compelled the king to demonstrate his commitment to the Palestine issue. These considerations explain why for forty years Amman rhetorically adopted Palestinian aspirations.

The king's dramatic but as yet partial cutting of ties with Palestine in July [1988] suggests that he now worries less about internal stability than about the dangers created by the West Bank imbroglio. Too, Jordan's recent disavowal of claims to sovereignty on the West Bank is a tactical twist that brings to mind similar declamations in the 1974-75 period. Husayn says he is deferring to the PLO; actually, he hopes to divide and destroy and then return. The nature of his conflict with the PLO remains unchanged.

Those who argue that Jordan-is-Palestine have been quick to dismiss Husayn's sincerity in order to protect their argument. However correct about Husayn, the general argument remains invalid, for it rips quotes to the effect that Palestine equals Jordan out of context. Just because Arab leaders have said so from time to time does not make this true.[175]

Mr Pipes concludes that 'Just because Arab leaders have said so from time to time does not make this true'. However, as Yehoshafat Harkabi, author of *Palestinians and Israel* notes:

> these at least depict the state of mind, controversies and aspirations of their formulators... [and] the statements themselves help explain motives for actions.[176]

[175] www.danielpipes.org/article/298, downloaded 11 May, 2007, and documented in his *Greater Syria: the History of an Ambition*, Oxford University Press USA, 1992

[176] *Palestinians and Israel,* Jerusalem: Keter Publishing House, 1974, pp. 131, 140

    Dancing in the Dragon's Jaws

Bibliography

Books

Arendt, Hannah. 1970. *Eichmann in Jerusalem*, New York: The Viking Press

— 2005. *Eichmann and the Holocaust*, London: Penguin Books.

Awad, Alex. 2001. *Through The Eyes of The Victims*, Bethlehem Bible College

Bierman, John. 1981. *Righteous Gentile (Raoul Wallenberg, Missing Hero of the Holocaust)*, Bungay, Suffolk: Penguin Books

Bleck, Rabbi Benjamin, 2004. *The Complete Idiot's Guide to Jewish History and Culture*, 2nd edition, Indianapolis: Alpha Books

Brother Andrew, 2005. *Light Force: the Only Hope for the Middle East*, London: Hodder & Stoughton

Bullock, Alan. 1975. *Hitler: a Study in Tyranny*, revised edition of 1962, London: Penguin Books

Burleigh, Michael. 2001. *The Third Reich - A New History*, London: Pan Macmillan

— 2006. *Sacred Causes (Religion and Politics From European Dictators To Al-Qaeda)*, London: HarperPress

Chacour, Elias. 1986. *Blood Brothers (A Palestinian's Struggle For Reconciliation In The Middle East"*, E. Sussex: Kingsway

Chilton, David. 1990. *The Days of Vengeance - An Exposition of the Book of Revelation*, Fort Worth: Dominion Press

Fisk, Robert. 2002. *Pity the Nation: the Abduction of Lebanon*, New York: Nation Books

— 2005. *The Great War for Civilisation: The Conquest of the Middle East*, London: Harper Collins

Gilbert, Sir Martin. 2007. *Churchill and the Jews*, London: Simon & Shuster

Gross, Jan T. 2000. *Neighbours: The Destruction of the Jewish Community in Jedwabne, Poland*, Princeton University Press

Guiness, Os. 1998. *The Call: Finding the Central Purpose of Your Life*, Nashville: Thomas Nelson

Hitler, Adolf. 1990. *Mein Kampf*, D.C. Watt (ed.), University of London

Josephus. *The Works of Josephus, "The Wars of the Jews"*, 1987 trans. William Whiston, Peabody, Mass.: Hendrickson Publishers

Katz, Arthur. 1998. *The Holocaust - Where Was God?* N.p.: Burning Bush Publications

Manchester, William. 1983. *The Last Lion (Winston Spencer Churchill - Visions of Glory, 1874-1932)*, New York: Dell Publishing

—   1988. *The Last Lion (Winston Spencer Churchill - Alone, 1932-1940)*, Boston, Toronto & London: Little, Brown & Co.

Michener, James. 1991. *The Source*, London: Transworld Publishers

Morris, Benny. 1988. *The Birth of the Palestinian Refugee Problem 1947-1949*, Cambridge University Press

Rees, Laurence. 2005. *Auschwitz: The Nazis and the Final Solution*, London: BBC Books

Rosenberg, Elliot. 1997. *But Were They Good For the Jews? (Over 150 Historical Figures From A Jewish Perspective)*, New York: Birch Lane Press

Ryan, Cornelius. 1984. *The Last Battle (Berlin 1945)*, Kent: New English Library

Said, Edward. 1992. *The Question of Palestine*, London: Vintage

Sereny, Gitta. 1995. *Albert Speer: His Battle With Truth*, London: Macmillan

Shirer, William. 1960. *The Rise and Fall of the Third Reich (A History of Nazi Germany)*, New York: Simon & Shuster

Speer, Albert. 1970. *Inside the Third Reich*, trans. Richard & Clara Winston, New York & Toronto: Mcmillan

—   2000. *Spandau: The Secret Diaries*, London: Phoenix Press

Steinberg, Milton. 1934. *The Making of the Modern Jew*, Indianapolis: Bobs-Merrill Co

Ten Boom, Corrie. 1982. *The Hiding Place*, New York: Random House

Timm, Angelika. 1997. *Jewish Claims Against East Germany (Moral Obligations and Pragmatic Policy)*, Budapest: Central European University Press

Treves, Sir Frederick. 1913. *The Land That is Desolate*, London: Smith, Elder & Co

Wiesel, Elie. 2006. *Night.* New York: Hill and Wang

Wright, N.T. 1996. *Jesus and the Victory of God*, Minneapolis: Fortress Press

Zertal, Idith. 2005. *Israel's Holocaust and The Politics of Nationhood*, Cambridge University Press

Books On-Line

Bosanquet, James. 1866. *Messiah the Prince*, London

Eusebius. 295-300 AD *Ecclesiastical History*, Caesarea

Josephus. 75-80 AD *The Wars of the Jews*, Rome

Twain, Mark. 1869. *Innocents Abroad*, New York

Bible Translations

New American Standard (NASB), La Habra, California: The Lockman Foundation, 1970

New International Version (NIV), Grand Rapids, Michigan: Zondervan Bible Publishers, 1978

New English Bible with the Apocrypha (NEB), New York: Oxford University Press, 1971

Newspapers & Magazines

Associated Press reports

Corriere della Sera, Rome

Olim Aid International newsletter

Time, "German Martyrs", 23 Dec 1940

New York Times

Websites Accessed

www.newprovidencebc.com/Mt%20Sinai/Biblical
    %20significance%20of%20Jabal%20al%20Lawz.pdf

www.catholic.com/thisrock/1997/9709chap.asp
    www.opusangelorum.org/Formation/Maryregina.html

www.ewtn.com/ENCYC/P9UBIPR2.HTM

www.restoringthevision.com/Ch12RtheV.htm

http://faculty.ucc.edu/egh-damerow/Statistics.html

www.religioustolerance.org/worldrel.htm

http://satucket.com/lectionary/Sudan.htm

http://www.jewfaq.org/whoisjew.htm

http://www.bc.edu/research/cjl/meta-elements/texts/cjrelations/
    resources/articles/cunningham_14Mar07.htm

http://www.biblical.edu/images/connect/PDFs/A%20Future
    %20for%20Israel.pdf http://mcadams.posc.mu.edu/txt/ah/
    tacitus/TacitusHistory05.html

http://members.aol.com/FlJosephus2/
    warChronology6Factions.htm

http://www.absoluteastronomy.com/topics/
    Hadrian#encyclopedia

www.aish.com/literacy/jewishhistory/CrashCoursePart44.asp

http://www.jewishvenice.org/ghetto/history.html

http://www.geocities.com/Athens/Academy/8636/History.html

http://www.jewishvirtuallibrary.org/jsource/vjw/Granada.html

http://www.jewishencyclopedia.com/view.jsp?
    artid=895&letter=C

www.fordham.edu/halsall/jewish/1348-jewsblackdeath.html

www.templeinstitute.org

http://www.mtwain.com/Innocents_Abroad

www.yad-vashem.org.il/visiting/sites/chambon.html

www.ethnologue.com/home.asp and ww.ethnologue.com/
    show_country.asp?name=PG

www.biblesociety.org/index2.htm

http://www.benisrael.org/site_content/principalburdens/
    frmst_principalburdens.htm

http://www.soundofegypt.com/palestinian/adult/
    massacres.htm#YASIN

http://www.danielpipes.org/article/298

http://www.kinghussein.gov.jo/his_palestine.html

www.un.org/unrwa/refugees/whois.html

www.mideastweb.org/palpop.htm

http://www.justiceforjews.com/index.html

http://www.nytimes.com/2007/11/05/world/middleeast/
    05nations.html?
    ex=1352005200&en=93fd256f53c21587&ei=5124&partner
    =permalink&exprod=permalink

http://wojac.com

www.asianews.it/index.php?art=1760&l=en

http://www.ccjr.us/dialogika-resources/primary-texts-from-the-
    history-of-the-relationship/272-luther-1523

http://focusonjerusalem.com/AbominationofDesolation.htm

http://www.abomination-of-desolation.com

Dictionaries & Encyclopaedias

Concise Oxford Dictionary. 1985. Oxford University Press.

Microsoft *Encarta 96* Encyclopaedia on CD-ROM

W.E. Vine's 1975 *Expository Dictionary of New Testament Words,*
    London: Oliphants

The Zondervan Pictorial Encyclopedia of the Bible. 1977.
    The Zondervan Corporation. Grand Rapids, Michigan

Jewish History Atlas, 1976. London: Weidenfeld & Nicolson.

Articles & Pamphlets

Ateek, Naim. 1995. *Biblical Perspectives on the Land* and A *Palestinian
    Perspective: The Bible and Liberation,* published in *Voices From The
    Margin* (ed. R.S. Sugirtharajah), New York: Orbis

Cunningham, Phillip A. 2007. *Reflections from a Roman Catholic
    on "Understanding Christian Support for Israel"*

Luther, Martin.1525. *Luther Against The Peasants*

— 1543. *The Jews And Their Lies*

Mangum, R Todd. 2008. *A Future For Israel In Covenant Theology; The Untold Story*

Prittie, Terence. 1975. *Middle East Refugees,* published in *The Palestinians,* New Brunswick, New Jersey: Transaction Books

Whittaker, Charles A. 2009. *The Biblical Significance ofJabal al-Lawz.*

Miscellaneous

CBS *60-Minutes* interview by Mike Wallace, aired February 6, 1983

Documents on German Foreign Policy 1918-1945, Series D, Vol XIII, London, 1964

Hitler, Speeches and Proclamations 2, Domarus (ed.), Wurzberg, 27 June 1937.

Hitler's Table Talk, 11 Aug 1942

Hitler, Adolf. *Political Testament,* Berlin, 1945

Nuremberg Trial Proceedings, Vol. 12, p. 318, Avalon Project, Yale Law School, April 19, 1946

Waltz with Bashir, animated documentary by Ari Folman, 2008

Index

Wound, in head and heel
    26-27. See also Bruise

Y

Yad Vashem 159
Yellow patches 151
Yugoslavia, treatment of Jews in
    20th Century 77-78

Z

Zeus 30, 110
Zion, daughter of, aka the
    nation of Israel 15-18. See
    also Mt Zion.
Zion, aka new Jerusalem 167,
    177

Other books by Graeme Carlé

Eating Sacred Cows
(A Closer Look at Tithing)

At a time when many of the Lord's people are burning out, this book is essential and refreshing, especially for those self-employed or in full-time ministry. Tithing was never supposed to be a church tax but to provide a holiday for the tither and their family and thereby reveal the goodness of God.

Because of the Angels
(Unveiling 1 Corinthians 11:2-16)

This text has been largely lost to today's church because we have badly misunderstood some of Paul's Hebrew presuppositions regarding 'head', 'covering', the fall of Satan and spiritual warfare. Liberating for men and women of God as it restores much needed revelation on gender differences and relationships as well as the mystery of the Nazarite vow.

The Red Heifer's Ashes
(Mysteries of Ancient Israel)

Considered by Orthodox rabbis to be the greatest mystery of the Law of Moses, this is an astonishing revelation of Messiah. Every detail is gently unfolded as the reader today follows a supernatural path through the whole of the Old Testament, just as the two disciples did on the road to Emmaus.

Born of the Spirit
(A study guide for new believers)

This interactive Bible study is for all who want to develop their personal spirituality by checking the foundations of what Jude the Lord's youngest brother called 'the faith which was once for all delivered to the saints' (Jude 3). Avoiding all denominational allegiances, find out for yourself how God wants us to love, live and learn.

These books are available from good bookstores or
Emmaus Road Publishing
PO Box 38 823 Howick, Auckland 2014 New Zealand
www.emmausroad.org.nz

Slouching Towards Bethlehem

The Rise of the Antichrists

Graeme Carlé

It is often thought today that the keys to understanding the Book of Revelation have been lost and are irretrievable but they're not. They were just buried under centuries of rubble created by the Gentile church's foolish attempts to distance itself from its Jewish foundations. If, like any archaeologist, we dig carefully we can rediscover them.

In *Dancing in the Dragon's Jaws,* we found one key to understanding Revelation chapter 12 is the metaphorical "time, times and half a time" and we unlocked the last 4,000 years of Jewish history.

Slouching Towards Bethlehem unlocks Revelation chapter 13 and the last 2,000 years of the Christian era, with startling results. Not only can we now understand the forces shaping history and the deaths of some 270 million in 20th Century genocides but we can also project the future of Israel and the Middle East.

Book 3 in the Revelation series

Gotta Serve Somebody

The Mystery of The Marks & 666

Graeme Carlé

Are you confused about 'The Mark of the Beast'?

You're not alone. The Mark and the number 666 have been controversial for centuries. Scholars and laymen alike have offered numerous interpretations, 'calculations' and wild guesses but most predictions have failed to materialize. Some say we just have to wait.

In this book, Graeme Carlé uses the keys recovered in the first two in his series (*Dancing in the Dragon's Jaws* and *Slouching Towards Bethlehem*) to unlock the symbols and 'times' of the most infamous and misunderstood mark in human history.

Instead of waiting for a world government or a global banking system that may never eventuate, Graeme believes and shows that The Mark is already here — and has been for the last 2,000 years! We've just not recognised it. It is actually the beast's counterpart of marks that God Himself placed on the forehead and hand of His people at the Exodus and in the wilderness, with a numbering system of names as described in the Book of Numbers.

We don't need a profound theological education or esoteric enlightenment but we do need a basic grasp of Jewish history and the Old Testament, as understood by 1st Century Jewish believers in Jesus of Nazareth.

Available from
Emmaus Road Publishing
PO Box 38 823 Howick, Auckland 2014 New Zealand
www.emmausroad.org.nz

ISBN 978-0-9582746-9-2

Book 4 in the Revelation series

Silencing the Witnesses

Jerusalem & The Ascent of Secularism

Graeme Carlé

Moses and Elijah back from the dead? The most popular interpretation of Revelation 11 today is literal – that Moses and Elijah are soon to reappear in the streets of Jerusalem as witnesses, to preach for three and a half years, then be killed by a metaphorical beast (a man called the Antichrist) before being resurrected again after three and a half days.

The most common academic view today, however, is that these are all metaphorical images, referring to the church being persecuted initially by the Romans, today by the whole world, but ultimately vindicated.

In this book, Graeme Carlé takes the metaphorical approach but from a Jewish perspective. The Early Church was, after all, led by Jewish disciples and/or Gentiles taught by Jewish disciples. He shows how the two witnesses would have been understood by John's 1st Century audience to be the Law and the Prophets, making essential connections with Jesus' parable of the rich man and Lazarus, and with Paul's two Jerusalems in Galatians 4.

In doing so, Graeme surveys the effects of the Law over 4,000 years of Jewish history, how it still applies to every Jew not under the New Covenant, and how it is relevant for all of us today.

ISBN 978-0-9941058-2-0

Graeme Carlé